UNIVERSITY OF WOLVERHAMPTON

05/07

Succeed at psychometric testing

PRACTICE TESTS FOR
NUMERICAL
REASONING
INTERMEDIATE LEVEL

New edition

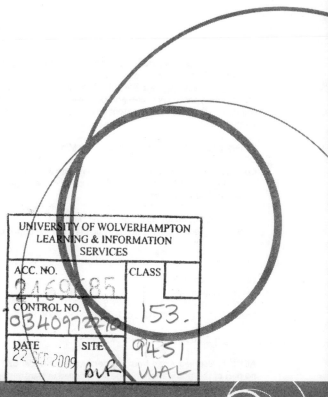

Succeed at psychometric testing

PRACTICE TESTS FOR
NUMERICAL
REASONING

INTERMEDIATE LEVEL

Bernice Walmsley

HODDER
EDUCATION
PART OF HACHETTE LIVRE UK

New edition

The publisher has used its best endeavours to ensure that the URLs for external websites referred to in this book are correct and active at the time of going to press. However, the publisher and the author have no responsibility for the websites and can make no guarantee that the site will remain live or that the content will remain relevant, decent or appropriate.

Orders: please contact Bookpoint Ltd, 130 Milton Park, Abingdon, Oxon OX14 4SB. Telephone: (44) 01235 827720. Fax: (44) 01235 400454. Lines are open from 9.00–5.00, Monday to Saturday, with a 24-hour message answering service. You can also order through our website www.hoddereducation.co.uk.

British Library Cataloguing in Publication Data
A catalogue record for this title is available from the British Library.

ISBN: 978 0 340 97227 4

First Published 2004
Second edition 2008
Impression number   10 9 8 7 6 5 4 3 2 1
Year   2012 2011 2010 2009 2008

Copyright © 2004, 2008 Bernice Walmsley

Typeset by Servis Filmsetting Ltd, Stockport, Cheshire.
Printed in Great Britain for Hodder Education, part of Hachette Livre UK, 338 Euston Road, London NW1 3BH by CPI Cox & Wyman, Reading, Berkshire, RG1 8EX.

Hachette Livre UK's policy is to use papers that are natural, renewable and recyclable products and made from wood grown in sustainable forests. The logging and manufacturing processes are expected to conform to the environmental regulations of the country of origin.

CONTENTS

ACKNOWLEDGEMENTS

With thanks to SHL for permission to reproduce the following material: Test 7, Questions 11–19 and 31–32; Test 8, Questions 21–30; Test 9, Questions 1–2 and Table 2.3; Test 9, Questions 6–8 and Figure 2.7; Test 9, Questions 16–18 and Figure 2.9.

FOREWORD

Should anyone tell you that a psychometric test will give an accurate indication of your level of intelligence, don't pay too much attention. It isn't necessarily true.

The credibility of the global psychometric testing industry rests on the belief of employers that a psychometric test will yield accurate and reliable data about a candidate's ability. Busy employers buy into the notion that a psychometric test will swiftly eliminate all the unsuitable candidates and deliver up only the best, brightest and most able candidates to the interview stage.

What is not widely known is that it is perfectly possibly for a candidate to drastically improve their own psychometric score by adopting a methodical approach to test preparation. The purpose of the *Succeed at Psychometric Testing* series is to provide you with the necessary tools for this purpose.

It is useful to know that a candidate's ability to perform well in a psychometric test is determined by a wide range of factors, aside from the difficulty of the questions in the test. External factors include the test environment and the professionalism of the test administrator; internal factors relate to the candidate's confidence level on the day, the amount of previous test practice the candidate has and the candidate's self-belief that they will succeed. While you cannot always control the external factors, you can manage many of the internal factors.

A common complaint from test takers is the lack of practice material available to them. The titles in the *Succeed at Psychometric Testing* series address this gap and the series is designed with you, the test taker in mind. The content focuses on practice and explanations rather than on the theory and science. The authors are all experienced test takers and understand the benefits of thorough test preparation. They have prepared the content with the test taker's priorities in mind. Research has shown us that test takers don't have much notice of their test, so they need lots of practice, right now, in an environment that simulates the real test as closely as possible.

In all the research for this series, I have met only one person who likes – or rather, doesn't mind – taking psychometric tests. This person is a highly successful and senior manager in the NHS and she has taken psychometric tests for many of the promotions for which she has applied. Her attitude to the process is sanguine: 'I have to do it, I can't get out of it and I want the promotion so I might as well get on with it.' She always does well. A positive mental attitude is absolutely crucial in preparing yourself for your upcoming test and will undoubtedly help you on the day. If you spend time practising beforehand and become familiar with the format of the test, you are already in charge of some of the factors that deter other candidates on the day.

It's worth bearing in mind that the skills you develop in test preparation will be useful to you in your everyday life and in your new job. For many people, test preparation is not the most joyful way to spend free time, but know that by doing so, you are not wasting your time.

The *Succeed at Psychometric Testing* series covers the whole spectrum of skills and tests presented by the major test publishers and will help you prepare for your numerical, verbal, logical, abstract and diagrammatic reasoning tests. The series now also includes a title on personality testing. This new title will help you understand the role that personality testing plays in both the recruitment process and explains how such tests can also help you to identify areas of work to which you, personally, are most suited. The structure of each title is designed to help you to mark your practice tests quickly and find an expert's explanation to the questions you have found difficult.

If you don't attain your best score at your first attempt, don't give up. Book yourself in to retake the test in a couple of months, go away and practise the tests again. Psychometric scores are not absolute and with practice, you can improve your score.

Good luck! Let us know how you get on.

Heidi Smith, Series Editor
educationenquiries@hodder.co.uk

Other titles in the series:

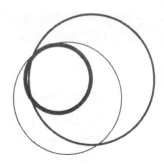

CHAPTER ONE
INTRODUCTION

WHO SHOULD READ THIS BOOK

This book is aimed at anyone who may have to take psychometric tests in the near future. You may have been called for an interview and heard that there will be a lot of tests. Or you may be applying for promotion and it has been mentioned that numerical ability will be important. Or you may be hoping to be accepted on a staff development programme in your company and know that tests will be used to whittle down the number of hopefuls. This prospect is, understandably, worrying. But it is certainly something that you can prepare for and by doing so improve your performance. This is the purpose of this book.

Make no mistake, it is possible to improve your score. Of course, the people who devise and publish these tests and the people who administer them don't publicise this fact. Publishers' sales depend on their clients believing that the results of the tests will guide them to the best candidates for the jobs on offer. The mystique of tests must be maintained.

There is no doubt that psychometric testing is not as straightforward as measuring your height or weight – your score may well change from day to day. Lots of factors will affect your performance, including lack of confidence, stress, the conditions in the testing venue and so on, so your test score on the day can only ever be an indication or estimation of your ability. This fact is sometimes forgotten and tests given greater credibility than perhaps they deserve but they are certainly something that you can prepare for and by doing so improve your performance. With practice you can get rid of some of the stress, lack of confidence and other barriers to success. In the next section we'll look at five factors that can affect your score on the day.

If you have been out of the education system for some years or you have been studying for a degree that has not demanded much use of the numerical skills you learned at school, you may have a dislike – or even a fear – of numbers. However, numerical reasoning tests are certainly something that you can prepare for and this preparation will improve your performance. Testing yourself on actual examples of the types of test that you will encounter is vital. Then, and only then, can you assess where your efforts to improve need to be concentrated.

In this book there will be a bit of theory about numerical tests and then plenty of practice. As we all know, 'practice makes perfect' – well, maybe not perfect, but practice will certainly improve your performance in this particular case. Practice can ensure that the peak of natural ability is reached when the test is taken.

Not only will you improve the scores you can achieve in these selection tests but the familiarity that comes from the extended practice available in this book will also raise your confidence level overall and this may help to improve your general performance at the interview. The main scope of this book is to provide you with sufficient samples of tests that you can use to prepare yourself. The confidence and familiarity, which will inevitably come with this amount of practice, is what will make the difference for you.

You will find lots of examples for you to work through and some handy tips on how to tackle them. We will be examining the common pitfalls associated with these tests and then discovering how to avoid them. Let's look first at the five factors that can affect your performance on the day.

HOW TO IMPROVE YOUR SCORE

Most graduates and applicants for jobs at a senior level (the people at whom this book is aimed) are not in any way innumerate. If they have problems with numerical tests, it is more likely to be due to a shortage of speed and accuracy or a lack of recent use of the vital skills than to a lack of ability.

The numerical knowledge that you will need to perform well in these tests is the maths you learned at school. It might be that you need a quick refresher course, but just as useful will be the sort of practice contained in this book and the explanations that accompany the answers to the questions. It is perfectly possible to improve your score by your own efforts. The aims of this book are therefore two-fold – to improve your performance in numerical tests by providing you with the practice you need and also to help you to lessen the impact of the factors that will affect your chances of success.

Before we go on to the main body of this book – the practice and explanations of mathematical problems – let's look at these factors that may affect your chances of success:

BELIEF IN YOUR ABILITY

This is about self-confidence. Research shows that a high expectation of success can be an important factor in getting a higher score. If you can get to the point where you know that you are well prepared and competent then you will improve your chances of success. This is because feeling confident increases the quantity of the type of hormones in your bloodstream that help you to focus. If, on the other hand, you're convinced that you will fail, then different hormones will make you anxious and less able to focus.

FAMILIARITY

Extensive evidence of the impact of coaching and practice for a variety of examinations shows that it improves performance dramatically. It may be that you have been sent some practice material by the people who will be administering your test. Inevitably, this will not involve many questions but it will show you what sort of questions you will have to deal with and you will be able to concentrate on the timed tests in this book that equate to the material received. Whatever the focus of the particular test that you are taking, the large quantity of practice questions in this book will certainly give you the advantage of familiarity.

SPEED

Speed rather than accuracy is what is most important in most psychometric tests that you will take – although it's worth saying here that wild guesses are very rarely useful. Speed is significant because tests are almost always based simply on the number you get right in a fixed amount of time and then your score is compared with a similar group of test-takers. Because of the way scores are evaluated and compared with others, only a slight improvement in your performance will dramatically improve your final evaluation. So, the more questions you answer the more chance you have of getting that vital extra point or two.

In view of the need for speed, the best advice is:

- always answer as many questions as possible
- go for speed not accuracy – but concentration is still essential, of course
- never spend too much time on any one question.

UNDERSTANDING

It is vital that you understand completely what is required of you in the test. You will not get a good score if you do not follow instructions and understand precisely what you are meant to do. For this reason it is worth practising the various types of test and, of course, reading the instructions carefully.

SURROUNDINGS

This is an element of the tests over which you have little control. Ideally, tests should be conducted in a quiet, comfortable area but it is not unknown for tests to be given in office corridors, open plan offices or 'spare' offices where the heating has been turned off or the phone keeps ringing. Practising at home may be good preparation for this eventuality as life will still go on around you while you are practising.

Having said that, the correct environment is certainly a factor in your getting the best score of which you are capable, so do not be afraid to complain if things are not right – it is likely that serious problems will be taken into account when assessing your performance if they are brought to the attention of the test administrator.

WHAT IS NUMERICAL REASONING?

Numerical reasoning is the ability to deal with numbers and to get useful information from them. When your aptitude in this area is being tested you will have to show that you can add, subtract, divide and multiply, work with fractions and percentages and probably also show your understanding of data in charts, tables and graphs. These are all skills that you will have been taught at school. Practice will help you to remember them.

Using this book will improve this ability to deal with numbers and help you to pass numerical reasoning tests. It does not mean that this book will help you to become a top mathematician capable of dealing with complex algebra or working out long division sums in your head. What you are aiming at is a basic understanding of the four arithmetical operations that you will use – addition, subtraction, multiplication and division.

This might not seem, at this stage, to be an enjoyable prospect – especially if you are typical of many adults who believe that they are 'no good at maths'. However, with practice and determination the tests will become easier and will then become less of a chore. They are a 'necessary evil' in today's competitive jobs market and the aim of this book is to ensure that you get sufficient practice to increase your chances of success.

WHY TEST NUMERICAL REASONING?

There is a common belief that, unless you are going to become an accountant or work in a bank, then you do not need to be 'good with numbers'. This is absolutely not the case. Just think for a moment about the real business world – here are just a few examples:

- sales people working out a deal with volume discounts and minimum orders
- a personnel officer dealing with pay increases
- an engineer planning a project
- taking cash from the public in a shop or restaurant
- working in a production department within a very tight budget or with measurement specifications for technical items

The examples of situations in which you need to be able to work with numbers are endless. And do not fall into the trap of thinking that, in this world where calculators are commonplace or where we have computers to help, you do not need to be able to work things out in your head. What about that sales person who needs to get an idea of what price he will accept in the middle of complex negotiations? Or the administration assistant receiving a batch of invoices, who could save a lot of time by knowing at a glance that the invoices are added up correctly. In the real world we are bombarded with numbers so we need to be able to use them efficiently and our prospective employers need to know that we have this ability.

From an employer's point of view, interviewing and taking on staff is an expensive and risky business. There are a number of ways in which aptitude tests can help:

- where a company has received a large number of applicants, tests can whittle down the number to a more manageable and cost effective level for interviewing
- tests can be combined with other selection procedures to enable the employer to make better recruitment decisions
- tests are much less subjective than interviews alone – this is better for the employer and for the interviewees
- better decisions at this stage will result in a lower staff turnover
- selecting the right employees will reduce wasted training
- reduction in the possibility of damage being done to a business by an incompetent member of staff
- CVs are notoriously unreliable. Anyone can declare that they are numerate – tests will show whether or not this is actually true.

These reasons make selecting staff by interview alone a very uncertain process and employers therefore look for more specific ways of proving whether or not the person they are interviewing has the ability to do the job. This is where aptitude tests, including ones that test numerical reasoning, become an extremely useful tool for an employer.

WHAT SORTS OF TESTS WILL YOU BE GIVEN?

The sets of aptitude tests given by employers may include ones to assess a variety of things such as your verbal reasoning or diagrammatic reasoning. However, our aim here is to concentrate on numerical reasoning.

Numerical reasoning tests will be timed and you will have to work quickly – but accurately. You will be told whether or not calculators are permissible and whether or not you are allowed to write on the question papers. The questions quite often have multiple-choice answers and you will be told how to indicate your answers. This may be by ticking or putting a cross in a space or sometimes by shading in a square or circle on the answer paper. This latter method is to facilitate computer marking in the case of large numbers of people taking the test. Whatever the instructions, it is vital that you follow them to the letter. If you are told to indicate your answer with a tick for example, do not put a cross. The person marking the test could possibly interpret this as your having deleted your answer to that question.

There are a number of different types of question that can be used to assess your aptitude for numbers:

- arithmetical
- number sequences
- tests based on graphs, charts and tables.

Each of these test types is intended to discover a different aspect of your ability to use numbers.

At this point, it will be helpful to explain the layout of the questions, answers and explanations included in this book. As you will see, there will be ten tests giving you plenty of practice at timed tests. After this there will be a chapter devoted to answers and explanations. This will include plenty of advice as to how you can tackle the questions and specific problems to look out for. You should note the correct answers and, even if you have got that one right, read the accompanying explanation. This is where the common pitfalls will be demonstrated and tips given on how to avoid them.

HOW TO USE THIS BOOK

As an introduction, we will look in a little more detail at the different types of questions.

1 ARITHMETICAL QUESTIONS

These are usually the most basic of the types of numerical reasoning test questions that will be encountered. They are based on arithmetical operations that most people will have learned and used throughout their school life. This is where practice might produce the most dramatic improvements.

Here is an example of this type of question:

Question: 19.8 × 5 (solve without using a calculator)

Answers:

a 92.1

b 95.0

c 99.0

d 80.0

e 100.0

Answer: c is correct.

Explanation: It is often easier to work out this type of calculation by rounding up or down to the nearest whole number. You can then get an approximate answer and quickly pick out the correct answer from the list of suggestions. So, in this example, you should round up 19.8 to 20, multiply by five and then, most importantly, remember that you rounded up and realise that the actual answer will be slightly less than the estimate of 100.

2 NUMBER SEQUENCES

This, as the name suggests, is a sequence of numbers where one or more numbers will be missing. It will be the interviewee's task to find it. Depending on the degree of difficulty of the sequence, finding the solution can become almost automatic. Consider your facility to count. Counting – adding one to each of the preceding numbers – is the first and most basic type of number sequence we learn. From being a difficult and almost incomprehensible process in our very early childhood, counting becomes something that, by the time we reach adulthood, we do automatically.

Here is an example of this type of question:

Question: Find the next number in the series 2, 5, 10, 17, 26, 37, ?

Answers:

a 45

b 55

c 40

d 50

e 10

Answer: d is correct.

Explanation: You should have spotted that this is a sequence adding increasing odd numbers to the preceding number to get the next one in the sequence – add 3, then 5, then 7 and so on. This is known as arithmetical progression. A slightly more difficult example of a number sequence would be geometric progression – where, for example, the sequence would proceed via a series of multiplications of the preceding number.

By working out the differences between the numbers you will see that each pair of numbers is separated by an uneven, increasing amount – a gap of three between the first pair, a gap of five between the second and third figures, an increase of seven from the third to the fourth number and so on. The next uneven number required at the end of the sequence is 13. Add 13 to the last figure and you will get the answer – 50.

Another type of question involving number sequences is error location. This is where you will have to find the inconsistency in the data. This can make candidates freeze or panic and might lead to a misunderstanding of the instructions. Take your time when reading the instructions and utilise the practice opportunities in this book. This will ensure a better result.

3 GRAPHS AND CHARTS

There are lots of different types of charts – everyone will be familiar with pie charts but have you ever seen a doughnut chart? It is just like a pie chart but, as you will have guessed, in the shape of a doughnut. There are also bar charts, column charts, line diagrams and sub-types within all of these categories.

For the purposes of your test, however, you are likely to meet only the main types – bar, column, line or pie charts. Examples of a column chart and a line chart are shown here, together with some questions and examples. The variety of information that can be presented in a graph, chart or table is enormous. For example, you could be presented with figures showing:

- examination test results
- employment statistics
- sales figures
- production figures.

Other popular information is that shown in many financial sections of newspapers – share prices and movements. All are given with the same aim and that is to test your ability to read the information shown in the charts or tables and to use it to come up with an answer. Your task in the test will therefore be to answer questions using the information presented in the chart. Examples of this type of question follow.

Use the **column chart** in Figure 1.1 to answer the following questions:

Question: How many more children than adults are taking piano lessons?

Answers:

   a 15

   b 5

   c 30

   d 10

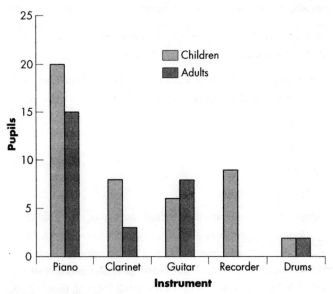

Figure 1.1 Column chart: music lessons

Answer: b is correct.

Explanation: Subtract the number of adults taking piano lessons from the number of children taking piano lessons (20 − 15 = 5).

Question: What is the total number of pupils receiving lessons?

Answers:

   a 60

   b 80

   c 73

   d 35

Answer: c is correct.

Explanation: Add together the number in every column – take care to include both children and adults.

Question: How many children are taking lessons in the instrument that is the least popular with adults?

Answers:

a 9

b 20

c 0

d 2

Answer: a is correct.

Explanation: First locate the instrument that is least popular with adults – the recorder – then read off the number of children taking lessons in that instrument.

Question: How many adults are taking lessons in the most popular instrument overall?

Answers:

a 8

b 25

c 15

d 35

Answer: c is correct.

Explanation: Care must be taken to give only the number of adults taking piano lessons and not the number of pupils overall who are taking piano lessons.

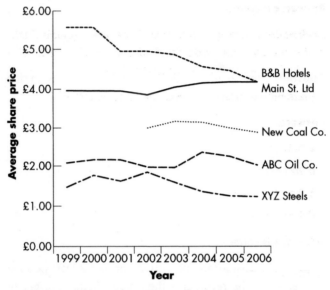

Figure 1.2 Line chart showing fluctuations in share prices

Use the **line chart** in Figure 1.2 to answer the following questions:

Question: Which company's shares were worth approximately half the value of those of Main Street Limited's in 1999?

Answers:

    a ABC Oil Co.

    b B&B Hotels

    c New Coal Co.

    d Main St. Ltd

    e XYZ Steels

Answer: a is correct.

Explanation: Here you should check the value of Main St. Ltd in the relevant year, divide this figure by two. That is £2.00 – then look for a share in 1999 priced at £2.00.

Question: Which company was first listed in 2002?

Answers:

   a ABC Oil Co.

   b B&B Hotels

   c New Coal Co.

   d Main St. Ltd

   e XYZ Steels

Answer: c is correct.

Explanation: The line representing the New Coal Company first appears in the chart in 2002.

Question: How much would 100 shares in New Coal Co. plus 100 shares in ABC Oil Co. have cost in total in 2003?

Answers:

   a £300

   b £5200

   c £520

   d £5.20

   e £52

Answer: c is correct.

Explanation: Be careful with this. The answers £5.20, £52 and £5200 are there to confuse. Add the two share prices together then make sure you multiply this total by 100.

Question: How much was the highest-priced share worth in 2002?

Answers:

   a £5.50

   b £2.00

   c £16.00

   d £6.00

   e £5.00

Answer: e is correct.

Explanation: This is simply a matter of reading off the value of the top-priced share in the relevant year. Do not add the share prices together or look at its highest price overall.

PROBLEMS AND PITFALLS

Having looked at the types of tests you may face and some of the specific ways in which you should answer them, we can now look at some of the more general problems and pitfalls associated with these tests. For example, you should always read the instructions carefully. Ask yourself a few questions as you read:

   • What exactly are you being asked to do?

   • Are you allowed to use a calculator?

- Can you write on the question paper?

- Or has some spare paper been supplied for the purpose of rough calculations?

- Do you need to estimate the answer?

There are also some pitfalls that are associated with specific types of questions. You will find many of these highlighted in this book when the individual questions are explained – see Chapter 3. Here are a few guidelines for avoiding some of the problems and pitfalls you may come across:

- Do not panic if you come across a negative number. Remember that -1 is still a number so it would still be a valid answer.

- A negative multiplied by a negative is always a positive (e.g. $-2 \times -2 = +4$).

- A negative number multiplied by a positive number is always a negative (e.g. $-2 \times 3 = -6$).

- If you come across figures enclosed in brackets, always try to solve the sum inside the brackets before going on to the rest of the question (e.g. $6 + (9 \times 5) = ?$ Work out $9 \times 5 = 45$ first, then add $6 = 51$).

- With tests where you have to write your answers on a separate sheet of paper, check from time to time that you are writing your answers in the right place. It is easy – especially if you have to miss out a difficult question or are working under time constraints – to continue down the answer sheet totally unaware that your answers are wrong simply because they are written in the wrong space.

- With number sequences you must work systematically. Work out the difference between the first and second numbers, then the second and third and so on. Consider the four arithmetical operations – add, subtract, multiply and divide – in turn.

- You must read and note the details given in the key to a diagram. If a figure for steel production of 10 is given, ask yourself '10 what?' – 10 tonnes, 10,000 tonnes? The answer to the question will be in the key.

THE VALUE OF PREPARATION

Unfamiliarity gets in the way of your natural ability, so practice is an invaluable form of preparation. Olympic runners do not just turn up at the track and set off as fast as they can – they will practise, treat their mind and body well and find out all they can about the race. Why should taking any other sort of test be different? So make the most of your period of preparation. Practice is the most important element of your preparation strategy. The timed tests in Chapter 2 will help with that. Aim to practise for up to two hours in any one session. Any more than that may be counterproductive. It is almost impossible to sustain the intense concentration needed for any longer than two hours. But what other forms of preparation should you consider?

Apart from the intensive practice that you can take advantage of by using the timed tests, there are other sorts of practice. For example, you should make yourself aware of the numbers that are all around you – and use them.

- When you are shopping in the supermarket, estimate what your total bill will be or continually calculate how much you can save by buying one product rather than another.

- Notice the data that is presented to you everyday in the financial pages of newspapers.

- Seek out numerical information in company reports or in trade magazines.

- Use train timetables to gain familiarity with using information presented in this way.

- Practise using currency exchange rates given in newspapers or by your travel agent.

- Brush up on using fractions, square roots, multiplication tables, percentages and decimals.

- Make sure you can use your calculator efficiently – you will not always be allowed to use one, but be prepared.

Above all, do not be afraid of numbers. If, after doing the tests in this book, you have specific concerns about your mathematical knowledge, get yourself a good, basic maths book and get yourself up to speed. Then practise until you are happy using numbers.

THE TEST ITSELF

Tests will be timed and not much time will be allowed for you to do the tests – it will be tight – and it is frequently not possible to complete all the tests in the time allotted. Do not let this worry you.

Even when you are sitting in the test room, you can still improve your chances of success. There are a few important things to remember at this stage:

- Listen to – and be sure to comply with – the instructions given by the test administrator
- Read the instructions on the test paper – these may cover items such as:
  - how much time you will be allowed
  - whether or not you may write on the margins of the test paper or if rough paper is supplied for your workings
  - whether you will be permitted to use a calculator
  - how you should indicate your answer – with a tick or a cross for example
  - what to do if you want to change one of your answers

Go through the questions methodically – do not be tempted to rush on to later questions first. Some papers are structured so that the questions get progressively more difficult – if you look at the later questions first, you may throw yourself into a panic.

If you do not understand something at this stage – before the test begins – speak up. There are sometimes example questions that you will be instructed to read before the timed test begins. Use the time allowed for this to ensure that you understand exactly what you are being asked to do. Do not try to pretend that you know everything – you do not need to impress the other candidates.

Read the questions carefully. Although you will be trying to work quickly, there is no point in answering all the questions but getting many of them wrong because you did not understand what was required.

STRATEGY

The main strategy during the test will involve timing – see below – but you may also want to consider how much you will use your powers of estimation. Here again, practice will help. Some questions on a numerical reasoning test are ideal for estimation. Rounding up or down can often be a quick way of arriving at the only possible answer from those given in multiple-choice questions. However, as noted above, take care if a system using negative scoring will be used – then accuracy is even more important. If you are really struggling with a particular question, do not waste time. Finding a difficult question can be unnerving. Far better to move on – there may be later questions that you find easy. Try not to let people around you affect your performance. Just because the person at the next desk to you has turned over a lot more pages than you, it does not mean that you are doing badly. They might have all their answers wrong!

TIMING

The time allowed for the various tests that you will undertake will range from about 5 to 15 minutes for an arithmetic test to maybe 40 minutes for a test involving charts and tables. If you are being tested on a number of aptitudes, the testing session may well take up to 2 hours in total.

The important thing is to use your time wisely. It is rare that too much time will be allowed for a numerical reasoning test. It is far more likely that you will run out of time. You will therefore need to work quickly whilst trying to be as accurate as possible. Try not to let one question take up too much of your time. If a particular question is proving difficult for you, move on. You could always come back to it if you find that you have plenty of time.

NOW TRY THE TESTS

Hopefully you are now convinced that preparation, including testing yourself using this book, will definitely improve your performance – and your chances of getting that job. So, on with the tests . . .

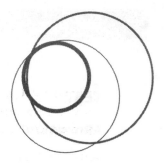

CHAPTER TWO
TIMED TESTS

You have learned a bit about various aspects of the tests that you might have to take and about preparing for them. Now we come to the most important part of this book – the timed tests. In the chapter of tests given in this book you will find a selection of the many types of questions that you will be asked. Work through these quickly but as accurately as possible, noting your answers and keeping a careful eye on the time allowed for each test. Try to make your practice sessions as close to a real test as possible. For instance, try to find somewhere that you can work undisturbed, only use your calculator where it is indicated that you may do so, record your answers in an organised way and use plenty of extra paper to do your rough calculations.

TEST 1

ARITHMETIC

(Answers to this test can be found on pages 135–142.)

Solve the following questions without using a calculator. For some of the questions there is a choice of five answers given. Only one of these is correct. Allow yourself 23 minutes.

1 $25 \times 5 = ?$

2 $29 \times 3 = ?$

3 $69 \div 3 = ?$

4 $100 \div 5 = ?$

5 $27 + 45 = ?$

6 $33 + 67 = ?$

7 $49 - 12 = ?$

8 $106 - 25 = ?$

9 $65 \times 3 = ?$

10 $27 \div 3 = ?$

The next batch of questions are multiple-choice – select the answer that you think is correct from the five choices given.

11 $19.8 \times 5 =$

  a 92.1

  b 95.0

  c 99.0

  d 80.0

  e 100.0

12 $8 \times 23 =$

  a 184

  b 181

  c 163

  d 188

  e 84

13 $16.4 + 7.1 =$

  a 33.5

  b 23.5

  c 15.3

  d 23.3

  e 13.8

14 $102 + 14 =$

  a 114

  b 88

  c 99

  d 96

  e 116

15 19.8 − 4.3 =

  a 16.1

  b 23.1

  c 15.1

  d 24.1

  e 15.5

16 116 + 88 =

  a 196

  b 204

  c 214

  d 184

  e 28

17 157 − 63 =

  a 94

  b 90

  c 68

  d 220

  e 97

18 $96 \div 3 =$

  a 27

  b 18

  c 33

  d 32

  e 23

19 $116.4 \div 4 =$

  a 92.1

  b 29.1

  c 29

  d 20

  e 30.1

20 $125 \div 5 =$

  a 25

  b 20

  c 15

  d 35

  e 29

21 If one ream of paper costs £3.99, how much would a box of five reams cost?

   a £20.00

   b £19.95

   c £25.95

   d £19.99

   e £39.90

22 The office stationery invoice is made up of £119.70 for copier paper, £23.50 for pens and pencils and £120.60 for printer cartridges plus £46.17 VAT. What would be the total invoice amount?

   a £409.97

   b £209.97

   c £263.80

   d £199.99

   e £309.97

23 Eight people work in your office with an average salary of £15,000. What would be the total annual salaries?

   a £150,000

   b £115,000

   c £120,000

   d £1875

   e £15,000

24 The working day is from 8.30 a.m. to 5 p.m. with half an hour for lunch. How many hours would be worked by each person from Monday to Friday inclusive?

a 20.0

b 35.5

c 35.0

d 37.5

e 40.0

25 The company sells six machines at £85,000 each. What is the total value of these sales?

a £5,100,000

b £42,500

c £425,000

d £510,000

e £51,000

26 One of your staff earns £15,000 per annum, pays £2500 in tax and £1465.00 in National Insurance contributions. What is the net pay?

a £11,035

b £12,500

c £11,000

d £1103.50

e £15,000

27 Your company has decided to pay out a total of £1500 in bonuses. If each of the twenty members of staff get an equal share of this, how much will each receive?

a £75.00

b £7.50

c £95.00

d £15.00

e £150.00

28 A customer makes a payment of £125,000. However, the outstanding amount on their account is only £79,000. By how much have they overpaid?

a £45,000

b £204,000

c £46,000

d £25,000

e £460

29 If each member of the workforce of 15 people works 2.5 hours overtime in a week, how much overtime in total will have been worked?

a 20.0

b 47.5

c 40.0

d 30.0

e 37.5

30 A discount of 10 per cent is offered on a machine priced at £85,000. What will be the discounted price?

a £93,500

b £85,000

c £76,500

d £80,000

e £67,500

31 $0.5 + 4.6 =$

a 1.5

b 5

c 5.1

d 6.1

e 9.6

32 $15 + 10 + 13 =$

a 30

b 35

c 28

d 18

e 38

33 71 − 29 =

a 42

b 100

c 200

d 79

e 99

34 144.4 − 5.6 =

a 390.8

b 140.8

c 128.8

d 150.1

e 138.8

35 242 × 7.5 =

a 1615

b 1815

c 1694

d 1494

e 1486

36 $22.2 \times 79.6 =$

  a 767.12

  b 1568

  c 1751.2

  d 1767

  e 1767.12

37 $6075 \div 5 =$

  a 1215

  b 1425

  c 1015

  d 121.5

  e 14.25

38 $44220 \div 22 =$

  a 2000

  b 2010

  c 2200

  d 20100

  e 2100

39 $16 \times 160 =$

  a 5260

  b 2260

  c 20560

  d 2560

  e 256

40 $806.35 - 200.18 =$

  a 606

  b 706.17

  c 6017

  d 6061

  e 606.17

TEST 2

PERCENTAGES, FRACTIONS AND SEQUENCES

(Answers to this test can be found on pages 142–150.)

Solve the following problems using a calculator if you wish. For some of the questions, there is a choice of five answers given. Only one of these answers is correct. Allow yourself 34 minutes.

1 20% of 500?

 a 100

 b 120

 c 200

 d 500

 e 400

2 45% of 200?

 a 45

 b 180

 c 90

 d 145

 e 100

3 $\frac{1}{5}$ as a decimal?

a 10

b 0.50

c 2.00

d 0.15

e 0.20

4 0.90 as a fraction?

a $\frac{9}{10}$

b 9.00

c $\frac{1}{10}$

d $\frac{1}{6}$

e $\frac{3}{4}$

5 $5x = 10$ so $x = ?$

a 50

b 15

c 1

d 500

e 2

6 $10x + 7 = 37$ so $x = ?$

a 17

b 3

c 5

d 30

e 7

7 $\frac{1}{6}$ of ? = 10

a 100

b 120

c 200

d 60

e 400

8 $\frac{1}{10}$ of 45?

a 4.5

b 45

c 450

d 55

e 5

9 $\frac{1}{8}$ of 152?

  a 20

  b 19

  c 133

  d 8

  e 18

10 15% of 80?

  a 100

  b 12

  c 95

  d 10

  e 50

11 Only a quarter of all the applicants for a job advertised are under 50 years old. If 224 people applied, how many are under 50?

12 Of 660 employees, 20 per cent are graduates. How many is this?

13 What percentage of £64.00 is £16.00?

14 If a worker earns £220 per week and is then given a five per cent increase, what will the new weekly wage be?

15 If nine out of ten workers drive to work, what percentage of workers do not drive to work?

16 A ream of paper used to cost £4.00 but now costs £4.20. By what percentage has the price increased?

17 A fifth of a factory's workers have received some training. If there are 100 workers in total, how many have not received any training?

18 If the average weekly wage is £320 but a worker only earns half of this, how much does he earn?

19 A quarter of a company's staff eat in the works canteen. If there are 408 workers, how many do not eat in the canteen?

20 There were 123 pens in the office stationery cupboard but a third have been given out. How many pens remain?

In the next group of ten questions, find the missing number indicated by a question mark.

21 2, 5, 10, 17, 26, 37, ?

  a 45

  b 55

  c 40

  d 50

  e 10

22 6, 13, ?, 27, 34, 41

  a 21

  b 20

  c 19

  d 18

  e 34

23 3, 9, 27, 81, 243, ?

   a 81

   b 727

   c 3

   d 747

   e 729

24 1, 2, 4, 8, 16, ?

   a 2

   b 32

   c 64

   d 50

   e 10

25 95, 85, 75, 65, 55, ?

   a 40

   b 55

   c 45

   d 50

   e 10

26 2, 5, 9, 14, 20, ?

  a 25

  b 29

  c 30

  d 23

  e 27

27 9, 16, 25, 36, 49, ?

  a 64

  b 49

  c 56

  d 63

  e 60

28 100, 96, 92, 88, 84, ?

  a 100

  b 90

  c 80

  d 78

  e 82

29 4, 7, 13, 22, 34, ?

  a 27

  b 49

  c 30

  d 37

  e 47

30 81, 76, 66, 61, 51, ?

  a 41

  b 46

  c 50

  d 66

  e 56

In the next ten questions, you are required to locate the error in the following number sequences – i.e. find the 'odd one out'.

31 5, 7, 9, 11, 12, 15

  a 5

  b 7

  c 11

  d 12

  e 15

32 35, 40, 50, 65, 80, 110

  a 40

  b 50

  c 80

  d 110

  e 65

33 12, 11, 8, 6, 4, 2

  a 11

  b 12

  c 2

  d 4

  e 6

34 6, 12, 17, 24, 30, 36

  a 6

  b 24

  c 30

  d 36

  e 17

35 100, 85, 70, 55, 50, 25

  a 50

  b 25

  c 85

  d 100

  e 70

36 129, 123, 115, 108, 101, 94

  a 115

  b 123

  c 129

  d 94

  e 108

37 3, 15, 75, 375, 1875, 8375

  a 8375

  b 1875

  c 375

  d 75

  e 3

38 4, 8, 16, 32, 40, 128

  a 4

  b 8

  c 16

  d 32

  e 40

39 93, 69, 51, 21, 25, 45

  a 45

  b 25

  c 21

  d 93

  e 69

40 7, 8, 10, 12, 17, 22

  a 7

  b 12

  c 8

  d 22

  e 17

TEST 3

INFORMATION FROM CHARTS AND TABLES

(Answers to this test can be found on pages 151–155.)

You should allow yourself 33 minutes for this test. You may use a calculator.

Using the facts and figures given in the statistical Table 2.1, answer the next five questions.

Table 2.1 Data on types of training

Type of training	2005	2006	2007
Clerical (%)	55	40	25
Managerial (%)	5	6	8
Technical (%)	40	25	33
IT Skills (%)	60	75	40
Other (%)	15	10	5
Not had any training (%)	12	25	30
Number of staff	250	300	280

1 In 2006, how many members of staff were given managerial training?

a 16

b 20

c 6

d 25

e 18

2 In 2007 approximately how many more staff were given technical training than in 2006?

a 17

b 25

c 19

d 25

e 8

3 How many more members of staff were there in 2006 than in 2005?

a 50%

b 20

c 50

d 17

e 30

4 What percentage of staff received clerical training in 2006?

a 25

b 30

c 120

d 55

e 40

5 In the year that 75% of staff received training in IT skills, how many people received clerical training?

a 300

b 120

c 40

d 25

e 70

The information contained in the pie charts in Figure 2.1 gives you all you need to answer the following five questions.

6 In percentage terms, by how much did the company improve its customers' stated intention to increase orders from 2005 to 2006?

a 19%

b 31%

c 7%

d 12%

e Cannot tell

7 In 2006, how many customers stated that they will decrease their orders?

a 15%

b 31

c 45

d 15

e Cannot tell

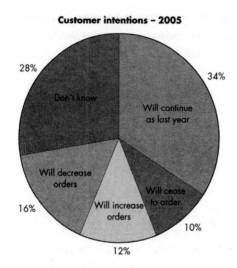

Customer intentions – 2005

28%

Don't know

34%

Will continue
as last year

Will decrease
orders

16%

Will increase
orders

Will cease
to order

10%

12%

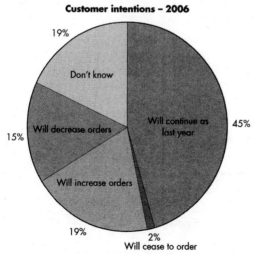

Customer intentions – 2006

19%

Don't know

Will decrease orders

15%

Will increase orders

Will continue as
last year

45%

19%

2%
Will cease to order

Figure 2.1 Pie charts showing results of customer surveys 2005/2006
(Number of customers surveyed in each year = 300)

8 What is the difference between the number of customers who said that they would 'continue as last year' in 2006 compared with 2005?

a 33

b 45

c 102

d 135

e 34

9 In 2005, how many customers in total expressed their intention to either cease to order from the company or to decrease their orders?

a 26

b 78

c 68

d 51

e Cannot tell

10 In 2006, how many more customers expressed their intention to 'continue as last year' than answered 'will cease to order'?

a 2

b 72

c 43

d 129

e 141

Use the information given in the chart in Figure 2.2 to answer the next five questions.

11 How much operating profit was made by the children's clothes manufacturing unit in the most profitable year for the company as a whole?

a £300,000

b £200,000

c £100,000

d £200

e £300

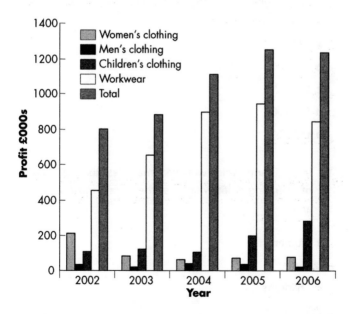

Figure 2.2 Column chart displaying data for operating profit of Clothing Unlimited by manufacturing area 2002–2006

12 Roughly what proportion of the total profit was represented by women's clothes in the least profitable year for the company as a whole?

  a 25%

  b 75%

  c 80%

  d 20%

  e £200,000

13 Approximately how much profit in total has been made by the children's clothes operating unit in the five years for which records are shown?

  a £800

  b £600,000

  c £600

  d £200,000

  e £800,000

14 In the year in which workwear made less than £500,000 of operating profit, which was the second most profitable area?

  a Women's

  b Men's

  c Children's

  d Workwear

  e Cannot tell

15 In the third most profitable year overall, approximately how much operating profit was made?

a £1,100,000

b £11,100,000

c £1100

d £900,000

e £1,200,000

Answer the next five questions using information contained in the line diagram in Figure 2.3.

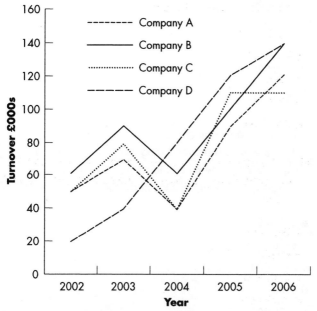

Figure 2.3 Line diagram comparing turnover figures for companies A, B, C and D (2002–2006)

16 Which of the four companies had the greatest increase in turnover between 2002 and 2005?

a Company A

b Company B

c Company C

d Company D

e Cannot tell

17 What was the total turnover of all four companies in 2006?

a £510,000

b £140,000

c £510

d £620,000

e £370,000

18 There was only one company that did not suffer a decrease in its turnover during the period shown in Figure 2.3. By how much did the turnover of that company rise between 2002 and 2006?

a £20,000

b £120

c £100,000

d £100

e £120,000

19 By how much did Company A's turnover differ from that of Company B in 2003?

a £50,000

b £30,000

c £20,000

d £10,000

e £40,000

20 Which company had the biggest fall in turnover between 2003 and 2004?

a Company A

b Company B

c Company C

d Company D

e Cannot tell

TEST 4

ARITHMETIC

(Answers to this test can be found on pages 156–160.)

Some questions in this test include a choice of five possible answers. You should try to find the only correct answer from this choice. Now complete the following arithmetic test without using a calculator. Allow yourself 23 minutes.

1 $24.4 \times 3 = ?$

2 $16 \times 0.5 = ?$

3 $25 \times 15 = ?$

4 $9 \div 4 = ?$

5 $143.5 \div 3.5 = ?$

6 $97.2 \div 3 = ?$

7 $8.14 + 3.75 = ?$

8 $131.3 + 99.8 = ?$

9 $17.6 + 29.3 = ?$

10 $137.6 - 94.8 = ?$

11 $297 \times 3 = ?$

a 900

b 96

c 100

d 300

e 891

12 $43.2 + 16.9 = ?$

  a 60

  b 60.1

  c 50.1

  d 40.1

  e 59.1

13 $29.1 \div 3 = ?$

  a 9.7

  b 9

  c 8.7

  d 11.7

  e 9.9

14 $98 \div 7 = ?$

  a 15

  b 13.9

  c 14

  d 13

  e 12

15 $107 \times 3 = ?$

  a 349

  b 321

  c 421

  d 121

  e 221

16 $41.1 + 106.9 = ?$

  a 149

  b 148

  c 148.9

  d 148.1

  e 149.1

17 $132 - 17 = ?$

  a 105

  b 125

  c 149

  d 115

  e 119

18 111.8 ÷ 10 = ?

   a 11.18

   b 1118

   c 1.118

   d 111.8

   e 11,180

19 14.2 × 20 = ?

   a 28.4

   b 2840

   c 7.1

   d 1404

   e 284

20 368 − 297 = ?

   a 91

   b 69

   c 71

   d 171

   e 103

21 If six friends go together to a restaurant and spend an average of £15.50 each, then share the bill equally between them, how much would they each have to pay?

a £20.00

b £15.50

c £15.00

d £31.00

e £93.00

22 If your restaurant bill comes to £47.50 and you decide to add a 10% tip, how much would you pay in total?

a £57.50

b £95.00

c £47.50

d £43.00

e £52.25

23 A machined part has a specified width of 630 mm and there is a tolerance of + or − 10%. What is the maximum width that would be acceptable?

a 693 mm

b 600 mm

c 650 mm

d 640 mm

e 567 mm

24 A printer produces four pages per minute. How long – in hours and minutes – would ten copies of a document consisting of 76 pages take to print?

a 1 hour 16 minutes

b 3 hours 10 minutes

c 190 minutes

d 304 minutes

e 76 minutes

25 If the cost of 9000 items is £3519.00, what is the cost of each item?

a 4.91p

b 3.91p

c 39.1p

d £0.39

e 4p

26 If there is a 15% discount on an order for 200 chairs at £16.50 each, how much would the total order cost?

a £2016.50

b £2970.00

c £1650

d £1402.50

e £2805.00

27 Four workers take $1\frac{1}{2}$ hours in total to pack an order. If only one worker was doing this job, how many hours would it take?

a 5 hours

b 4 hours

c 6 hours

d $1\frac{1}{2}$ hours

e 10 hours

28 One machine part costs £16.55. How much would 100 of these parts cost?

a £1655.00

b £165.50

c £16,550

d £1655.50

e £1.65

29 A salesman receives commission of £0.80 for every item he sells. If he sells 4000 items, how much will his commission payment be?

a £800

b £1600

c £320

d £3200

e £1632

30 A worker produces 127 items but 9 are rejected. How many are accepted?

a 117

b 119

c 127

d 118

e 136

31 $(16 - 11) + 21 = ?$

a 22

b 26

c 24

d 48

e 46

32 $(1.3 \times 9) \div 7 = ?$

a 0.2

b 1.5

c 16.71

d 2

e 1.67

33 $47 \times 5.3 = ?$

 a 294.1

 b 241

 c 250

 d 249.1

 e 24.91

34 $1438 \div 2.4 = ?$

 a 599.2

 b 600

 c 59.9

 d 499

 e 500

35 $97 \times 41 = ?$

 a 3975

 b 3977

 c 4000

 d 4025

 e 3797

36 $(127 + 38) \div 1.5 = ?$

   a 110

   b 1100

   c 11.0

   d 165

   e 120

37 $903.4 - 2.18 = ?$

   a 901.3

   b 900.22

   c 901.22

   d 899.22

   e 900.3

38 $15 \times 150 = ?$

   a 225

   b 2250

   c 2050

   d 2200

   e 2150

39 $(163 + 2.8) \times 4 = ?$

  a 660

  b 663.2

  c 664

  d 6.63

  e 6632

40 $29701 \div 7 = ?$

  a 4343

  b 4342

  c 4242

  d 4324

  e 4243

TEST 5

PERCENTAGES, FRACTIONS AND SEQUENCES

(Answers to this test can be found on pages 160–165.)

Solve the following problems without using a calculator. Select your answer from the five answers shown. Only one of these is correct. Allow yourself 29 minutes.

1 What is the VAT (at 17.5%) on an article costing £19.99?

a £4.00

b £3.99

c £3.50

d £3.00

e £4.97

2 What is 25% discount on a machine part costing £37.60?

a £10.00

b £9.40

c £10.40

d £8.49

e £3.76

3 $12\frac{1}{2}$% of 400?

a 100

b 75

c 50

d 80

e 25

4 95% of 1000?

a 95

b 950

c 800

d 850

e 80

5 $\frac{1}{6}$ of 66.6?

a 11.6

b 12

c 72

d 11.1

e 111

6 400% of £10

a £100

b £40

c £400

d £4

e £0.40

7 0.2 as a fraction?

a $\frac{1}{6}$

b $\frac{1}{2}$

c $\frac{1}{10}$

d $\frac{1}{5}$

e $\frac{1}{4}$

8 $\frac{1}{3}$ of 450?

a 150

b 300

c 400

d 200

e 125

9 $10\frac{2}{3} - 1\frac{1}{6} = ?$

a $9\frac{1}{3}$

b $10\frac{1}{3}$

c $9\frac{1}{6}$

d $9\frac{2}{3}$

e $9\frac{1}{2}$

10 $15\frac{1}{2} + 21\frac{3}{4} = ?$

a $27\frac{1}{4}$

b $37\frac{1}{2}$

c $36\frac{1}{4}$

d $37\frac{1}{4}$

e $37\frac{3}{4}$

11 What is $\frac{1}{25}$ as a percentage?

a 10%

b 25%

c 4%

d 20%

e 6%

12 Express 45% as a fraction in its simplest form.

  a $\frac{9}{10}$

  b $\frac{45}{100}$

  c $\frac{1}{2}$

  d $\frac{9}{20}$

  e $\frac{2}{5}$

13 $\frac{3}{8} + \frac{5}{16} = ?$

  a $\frac{11}{16}$

  b $\frac{8}{16}$

  c $\frac{1}{2}$

  d $\frac{8}{24}$

  e $\frac{2}{3}$

14 $\frac{1}{2} + \frac{1}{3} = ?$

  a $\frac{2}{5}$

  b $\frac{2}{3}$

  c $\frac{9}{10}$

  d $\frac{5}{6}$

  e 1

15 Express $\frac{2}{5}$ as a percentage.

  a 20%

  b 40%

  c 25%

  d 15%

  e 45%

16 If rail ticket prices go up by 5%, how much would the new price of a ticket be if it costs £45.00 before the increase?

  a £47.25

  b £50.00

  c £48.00

  d £2.25

  e £46.50

17 A third of a company's 210 employees are members of their healthcare scheme. How many is this?

  a 21

  b 140

  c 80

  d 70

  e 60

18 A company surveys its employees and finds that 60% are in favour of flexible working hours while a further 15% are against. The remainder did not respond to the survey. Of 400 employees, how many did not respond?

a 240

b 100

c 60

d 300

e 125

19 Half of a company's invoices are paid on time and a third are paid a month late. The remainder are still outstanding. Of a total invoice value of £360,000, what is the value of the invoices that have been paid?

a £25,000

b £250,000

c £30,000

d £36,000

e £300,000

20 Only 1 in 10 of a company's workers have been with the company for over 5 years. If 25% have been with the company less than 1 year, what percentage have been there between 1 and 5 years?

  a 75%

  b 65%

  c 10%

  d 25%

  e 50%

In the next ten questions, you are required to find the missing number indicated by a question mark (without using a calculator). Indicate your choice of answer from those given, only one of which is correct.

21 623, 604, 585, 566, 547, ?

  a 528

  b 428

  c 258

  d 570

  e 567

22 431, 452, 473, 494, 515, ?

  a 538

  b 546

  c 555

  d 536

  e 535

23 69, 70, 72, 76, 84, 100, ?

  a 132

  b 200

  c 164

  d 105

  e 119

24 27, 36, 45, 54, 63, ?

  a 69

  b 70

  c 71

  d 72

  e 73

25 97, 94, 88, 79, 67, ?

  a 53

  b 54

  c 50

  d 51

  e 52

26 78125, 15625, 3125, 625, 125, ?

  a 30

  b 25

  c 20

  d 250

  e 200

27 28, 35, 42, ?, 56, 63

  a 45

  b 49

  c 50

  d 48

  e 51

28 16, 18, 21, 25, 30, ?

   a 37

   b 32

   c 34

   d 36

   e 38

29 3, 9, 27, 81, 243, ?

   a 729

   b 727

   c 547

   d 529

   e 486

30 400, 375, 350, 325, ?, 275

   a 310

   b 305

   c 300

   d 260

   e 290

The final five questions in this test require you to find the error in the following number sequences – the 'odd one out'. Indicate your choice of answer from those given, only one of which is correct.

31 63, 54, 45, 34, 27, 18

  a 18

  b 27

  c 34

  d 45

  e 54

32 128, 100, 121, 98, 119, 96

  a 96

  b 128

  c 121

  d 100

  e 119

33 7, 14, 28, 56, 112, 220

  a 14

  b 28

  c 56

  d 112

  e 220

34 16, 18, 22, 24, 36, 46

  a 16

  b 18

  c 22

  d 24

  e 36

35 25, 40, 55, 65, 85, 100

  a 25

  b 40

  c 55

  d 65

  e 85

TEST 6

INFORMATION FROM CHARTS AND TABLES

(Answers to this test can be found on pages 166–169.)

All the questions in this test are multiple-choice. Indicate your answer from those suggested. You may use a calculator. Allow yourself 28 minutes.

Use the facts and figures given in the statistical Table 2.2 to answer the next five questions.

Table 2.2 Exhibition attendance

Category of exhibitor	No. of exhibitors in category	No. of visitors logged
Catering companies	25	188
Packaging suppliers	6	62
Distributors	7	30
Cash and carry outlets	9	45
Irish Food Board	1	263

1 The figures shown in Table 2.2 refer to visitors during the last day of the exhibition. If attendance was 20% higher on the previous day, how many visitors did the distributors receive on that day?

a 24

b 6

c 35

d 36

e 20

2 What was the total number of visitors logged?

a 488

b 48

c 588

d 263

e 608

3 If the number of exhibitors is increased by a half the following year, how many exhibitors would there be?

a 24

b 72

c 48

d 50

e 70

4 Which category of exhibitor had the second highest number of visitors?

a Catering

b Packaging

c Distributors

d Cash and carry

e Irish Food Board

5 Which two categories had a total of 13 exhibitors?

a Catering and cash and carry

b Packaging and distributors

c Cash and carry and distributors

d Distributors and catering

e Catering and packaging

The pie charts in Figure 2.4 give you all the information you need to answer the following ten questions.

6 How many more permanent members of production staff than temporary production staff were employed?

a 26

b 30

c 130

d 10

e 100

7 How many people were employed in total in the accounts department?

a 20

b 45

c 40

d 50

e 11

(a) Temporary staff (total employed = 190)

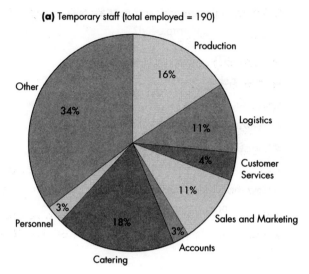

(b) Permanent staff (total employed = 500)

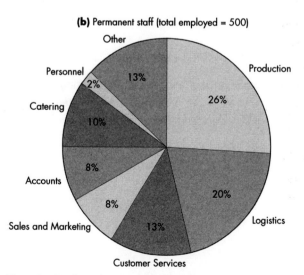

Figure 2.4 Pie charts showing number of staff employed in 2006

8 Which single category accounts for over a third of all temporary staff employed?

a Production

b Personnel

c Other

d Sales and Marketing

e Logistics

9 How many permanent staff, in total, are not employed in Production?

a 500

b 60

c 190

d 370

e 630

10 The Customer Services and Sales and Marketing departments are to be combined. How many temporary staff would be employed in the new department?

a 162

b 20

c 28

d 8

e 105

11 Which department employs the largest percentage of permanent employees?

a Other

b Production

c Logistics

d Sales and Marketing

e Customer Services

12 A fifth of permanent staff are employed in Logistics. How many is this?

a 100

b 200

c 20

d 45

e 65

13 How many more permanent than temporary staff are employed?

a 190

b 690

c 310

d 500

e 300

14 Which two departments employ 6% of temporary staff?

a Accounts and Other

b Customer Services and Personnel

c Customer Services and Accounts

d Personnel and Accounts

e Production and Logistics

15 Which department employs the smallest percentage of permanent staff?

a Personnel

b Catering

c Accounts

d Sales and Marketing

e Logistics

Now use the information given in the chart in Figure 2.5 to answer the following five questions.

16 You can see that club membership of monthly-paid staff has increased year on year. In which year did the number of monthly-paid staff members first exceed that of weekly-paid staff?

a 2002

b 2003

c 2004

d 2005

e 2006

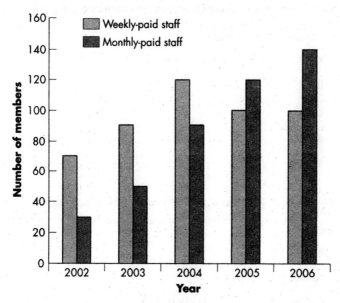

Figure 2.5 Column chart – social club membership 2002–2006

17 How many members in total were there in 2003?

  a 45

  b 50

  c 85

  d 90

  e 140

18 How many more monthly-paid staff members were there in 2006 than in 2002?

  a 110

  b 90

  c 140

  d 30

  e 60

19 In which year was there the smallest difference between the numbers of members of the two categories of staff?

  a 2002

  b 2003

  c 2004

  d 2005

  e 2006

20 In which year did the membership of weekly-paid staff show a decrease?

  a 2002

  b 2003

  c 2004

  d 2005

  e 2006

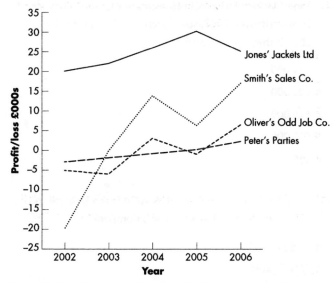

Figure 2.6 Line diagram – profit and loss data for start-up companies

Answer the following five questions using information contained in the line diagram in Figure 2.6.

21 In which year did Smith's Sales Company show a profit for the first time?

a 2002

b 2003

c 2004

d 2005

e 2006

22 Jones' Jackets Ltd expect to increase their 2006 profit by 20% in the next year. How much will their profits be in 2007 if they are successful?

a £30,000

b £25,000

c £20,000

d £35,000

e £30

23 In the years from 2002 to 2006, what is the total net profit or loss made by Oliver's Odd Job Company?

a £9000 profit

b £6000 profit

c £10,000 profit

d £3000 profit

e £3000 loss

24 Which company, if any, continually improved its profit and loss figures year on year?

a Smith's Sales Co.

b Jones' Jackets Ltd

c Peter's Parties

d Oliver's Odd Job Co.

e None

25 Which company improved its profit figure by the largest amount in any one year of trading?

a Smith's Sales Co.

b Jones' Jackets Ltd

c Peter's Parties

d Oliver's Odd Job Co.

e Cannot tell

TEST 7

ARITHMETIC

(Answers to this test can be found on pages 169–175.)

Solve the following questions without using a calculator. Allow yourself 22 minutes.

1 $45 \times 3 = ?$

2 $29 - 29 = ?$

3 $65 \div 5 = ?$

4 $63 \div 9 = ?$

5 $123 - 111 = ?$

6 $529 - 32 = ?$

7 $84 \div 7 = ?$

8 $349 + 62 = ?$

9 $9 + 27 = ?$

10 $16 \times 4 = ?$

11 $23 + 58 = ?$

 a 71

 b 81

 c 85

 d 91

 e 95

12 $28 \div 4 = ?$

  a 5

  b 6

  c 7

  d 8

  e 9

13 $? = 1.5 \times 2.5$

  a 2.5

  b 2.75

  c 3.00

  d 3.5

  e 3.75

14 $68 - 29 = 114 - ?$

  a 39

  b 65

  c 68

  d 75

  e 85

15 $\frac{1}{3} - \frac{1}{5} = ?$

a $\frac{1}{15}$

b $\frac{1}{8}$

c $\frac{2}{15}$

d $\frac{1}{2}$

e $\frac{3}{5}$

16 $17 \times ? = 204$

a 9

b 10

c 11

d 12

e 13

17 $132 \div ? = 12$

a 9

b 9.5

c 10

d 10.5

e 11

18 16 + 25 = ? + 13

 a 28

 b 31

 c 38

 d 41

 e 48

19 21 ÷ 3 = 91 ÷ ?

 a 7

 b 9

 c 11

 d 12

 e 13

20 49 ÷ 3.5 = ?

 a 7

 b 14

 c 21

 d 13

 e 15

21 Twelve boxes of spare parts weigh 144 kilos. How much do three boxes weigh?

a 12 kg

b 36 kg

c 24 kg

d 40 kg

e 20 kg

22 A collection for a colleague's retirement gift yields £81. If there are 27 members of staff, what was the average contribution?

a £2

b £9

c £5

d £3

e £4

23 A company spends an average of £128 per month on stationery. How much is its annual stationery bill?

a £1336

b £1563

c £536

d £1536

e £1530

24 The cost of a plane ticket to Paris was £145 plus tax of
£10. If your taxi to the airport was £23, how much did the
journey cost in total?

  a £180

  b £155

  c £118

  d £176

  e £178

25 A company has sales of £210,000. If the wholesale cost of
the goods was £100,000 and delivery charges totalled
£12,000, how much profit did it make?

  a £98,000

  b £100,000

  c £102,000

  d £9800

  e £108,000

26 A man is 6″ taller than his son who is 5′8″ tall. How tall is
the man?

  a 5′10″

  b 6′

  c 6′2″

  d 6′4″

  e 6′1″

27 A man works for $3\frac{1}{2}$ hours then takes a break of 45 minutes. He then works for a further 3 hours and drives for 1 hour to get home. How long did he spend working?

a $8\frac{1}{4}$ hours

b $7\frac{1}{2}$ hours

c $7\frac{1}{4}$ hours

d 6 hours

e $6\frac{1}{2}$ hours

28 If a decorator has 15 litres of paint, how many rooms can he/she paint if each room takes 2.5 litres?

a 12

b 6

c 9

d 15

e 3

29 If a three-minute phone call to Australia costs 85 pence, how much would a 15-minute call cost?

a £3.50

b £3.75

c £4.00

d £4.25

e £4.50

30 A company pays a deposit of £7500 on a machine costing £70,000. What is the balance outstanding?

  a £60,000

  b £77,500

  c £63,000

  d £62,500

  e £52,500

The next ten questions are numerical problems to which you must estimate the answers. Note the word ESTIMATE. For each question you are required to choose the answer, from the five answers given, which is nearest to your estimate.

31 $24 \times 0.8 = ?$

  a 16

  b 220

  c 19

  d 24

  e 140

32 76% of 156 = ?

  a 120

  b 160

  c 140

  d 100

  e 180

33 $\frac{1}{5}$ of 29 = ?

  a 34

  b 5

  c 8

  d 4

  e 6

34 $1.4 \times 40 = ?$

  a 60

  b 56

  c 64

  d 44

  e 160

35 $571 + 1307 = ?$

  a 1900

  b 1800

  c 2000

  d 1700

  e 700

36 $401 - 903 = ?$

   a 1300

   b 500

   c -500

   d -400

   e -1300

37 50% of 9389 = ?

   a 3700

   b 3900

   c 3700

   d 4700

   e 5000

38 £29.83 + £47.21 = ?

   a £75

   b £76

   c £80

   d £29

   e £85

39 89% of 1208 = ?

   a 1180

   b 1008

   c 1120

   d 1080

   e 1200

40 $\frac{3}{16}$ of £20 = ?

   a £3.75

   b £5.50

   c £5.25

   d £4.20

   e £4.00

TEST 8

PERCENTAGES, FRACTIONS AND SEQUENCES

(Answers to this test can be found on pages 175–179.)

Solve the following questions without using a calculator. Allow yourself 34 minutes.

1 8 = what percentage of 32?

  a 10

  b 50

  c 20

  d 30

  e 25

2 What is 50% of $\frac{1}{2}$?

  a $\frac{1}{2}$

  b $\frac{1}{4}$

  c $\frac{1}{3}$

  d $\frac{1}{10}$

  e $\frac{1}{5}$

3 10% of 0.1 = ?

  a 1.0

  b 10.0

  c 0.01

  d 0.2

  e 0.1

4 $\frac{1}{4} + \frac{1}{2} + \frac{1}{8} = ?$

  a $\frac{5}{8}$

  b $\frac{2}{3}$

  c $\frac{3}{4}$

  d $\frac{7}{8}$

  e 1

5 10% of 50% of 400 ?

  a 60

  b 40

  c 20

  d 100

  e 50

6 $\frac{2}{5}$ of 10125 = ?

  a 4050

  b 4000

  c 3950

  d 4025

  e 2025

7 40% of £230 = ?

a £88

b £92

c £90

d £94

e £86

8 £110 + 5% = ?

a £125.00

b £110.50

c £115.00

d £120.00

e £115.50

9 Two ninths of 81?

a 9

b 18

c 27

d 10

e 11

10 $(\frac{1}{3} + \frac{2}{9}) \times 3 = ?$

  a $3\frac{2}{9}$

  b $\frac{2}{3}$

  c $1\frac{2}{3}$

  d $1\frac{1}{3}$

  e 3

11 50% of a company's workers are below average height. If the company employs 126 people, how many are shorter than average?

12 If a Production Department manufactures 3000 machine parts but only 80% are of the required quality, how many have to be rejected?

13 A survey of your 123 customers shows that a third of them are unlikely to place further orders with you. How many is this?

14 A modification to your printer results in a 10% reduction in printing time. If 46 pages took 10 minutes prior to the modification, how long would it now take to print 46 pages?

15 A new pack of pens has two free pens. The original pack had 50 pens, so what percentage do the two free ones represent?

16 If one printer costs £50 but a discount of 10% is available if you buy two, how much would two printers cost in total?

17 Your stationery supplier reduces all his prices by $12\frac{1}{2}$%. How much would your usual monthly order of £128 cost after this reduction?

18 75% of a company's employees are female. Of a total workforce of 1244, how many are male?

19 A manager spends two fifths of his £120,000 monthly budget on salaries. How much is this?

20 If you work 8 out of 24 hours, what fraction of the day do you work?

Now find the missing number indicated by a question mark in the next ten questions (without using a calculator).

21 2, ?, 8, 16, 32, 64

  a 3

  b 4

  c 5

  d 6

  e 7

22 15, 13, ?, 9, 7, 5

  a 10

  b 11

  c 12

  d 13

  e 14

23 $\frac{1}{3}, \frac{2}{6}, \frac{3}{9}, \frac{4}{12}$, ?

a $\frac{5}{12}$

b $\frac{5}{13}$

c $\frac{5}{15}$

d $\frac{6}{15}$

e $\frac{6}{16}$

24 1.5, 3.0, 4.5, ?, 7.5

a 5

b 5.5

c 6

d 6.5

e 7

25 3, 4, 6, 7, ?, 10

a 9

b 10

c 11

d 12

e 13

26 ?, 14, 12, 11, 11, 12

   a 13

   b 15

   c 16

   d 17

   e 28

27 4, 10, 18, ?, 40, 54

   a 28

   b 30

   c 32

   d 34

   e 36

28 2, 4, 8, 10, 20, ?, 44

   a 22

   b 24

   c 28

   d 36

   e 40

29 2, 3, 5, 8, ?, 21

  a 9

  b 11

  c 13

  d 15

  e 17

30 2, 3, 1, 4, 0, 5, ?

  a −1

  b 0

  c 1

  d 2

  e 3

Next, find the error in the following ten number sequences – the 'odd one out'.

31 1, 3, 6, 7, 9, 11

  a 1

  b 3

  c 6

  d 7

  e 9

32 93, 96, 100, 104, 111, 118

  a 93

  b 96

  c 100

  d 104

  e 111

33 4601, 4590, 4578, 4565, 4551, 4535

  a 4551

  b 4590

  c 4578

  d 4535

  e 4565

34 $-4, -3, -2, -1, 0, +2$

  a -3

  b -2

  c -1

  d 0

  e $+2$

35 8, 4, 16, 8, 36, 16

   a 16
   b 36
   c 8
   d 16
   e 4

36 1, 2, 6, 24, 120, 620

   a 620
   b 120
   c 24
   d 6
   e 2

37 2, 6, 12, 17, 34, 39

   a 39
   b 2
   c 6
   d 34
   e 12

38 0, 1, 4, 6, 10, 15

  a 0

  b 1

  c 4

  d 6

  e 10

39 19, 23, 27, 31, 35, 41

  a 19

  b 27

  c 35

  d 41

  e 23

40 15, 12, 10, 8, 5, 2

  a 2

  b 10

  c 8

  d 5

  e 12

TEST 9

INFORMATION FROM CHARTS AND TABLES

(Answers to this test can be found on pages 179–182.)

You may use a calculator for this test. Allow yourself 25 minutes.

Using the facts and figures given in Table 2.3, answer the five questions below.

Table 2.3 Telephone calls received by customer services this month

Person taking call	No. of product enquiries	No. of complaints	No. of accounts queries	Total no. of calls
Jo	155	6	6	167
Mark	310	2	10	322
Michelle	205	0	47	252
Susan	112	14	25	151
Tony	370	8	35	413

1 How many product enquiries were received this month?

a 1142

b 1152

c 1182

d 1232

e 1292

2 If each complaint call lasted for an average of 12 minutes, how much time was spent dealing with complaint calls?

a 5 hours 12 minutes

b 5 hours 24 minutes

c 5 hours 36 minutes

d 5 hours 48 minutes

e 6 hours

3 How many complaint calls were dealt with, excluding the calls that Susan handled?

a 22

b 14

c 8

d 10

e 16

4 How many more calls in total than Jo did Mark handle?

a 167

b 155

c 322

d 255

e 55

5 Who dealt with the greatest number of product enquiries?

a Jo

b Mark

c Michelle

d Susan

e Tony

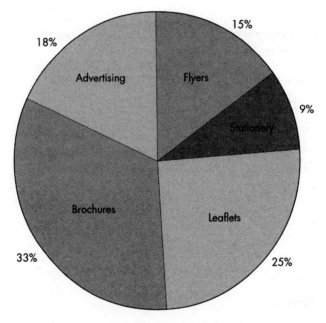

Figure 2.7 Cost of promotional activities in last financial year (total cost over year = £80,000)

The information contained in the pie chart in Figure 2.7 gives you all you need to answer the following five questions.

6 How much money was spent on promotional stationery in the last financial year?

a £4,900

b £5,300

c £6,800

d £7,200

e £7,400

7 If 50,000 brochures were printed, what was the approximate cost per brochure?

a 26p

b 44p

c 53p

d 62p

e 78p

8 If the average cost of printing a flyer is 4p, how many were printed in the last financial year?

a 200,000

b 300,000

c 400,000

d 600,000

e 900,000

9 Which type of promotional activity accounted for one quarter of the amount spent last year?

a Advertising

b Flyers

c Stationery

d Leaflets

e Brochures

10 If the budget is increased by 10% for the forthcoming year, how much will the new budget be?

a £88,000

b £80,000

c £8,000

d £10,000

e £80,800

Now use the information given in the chart in Figure 2.8 to answer the following five questions.

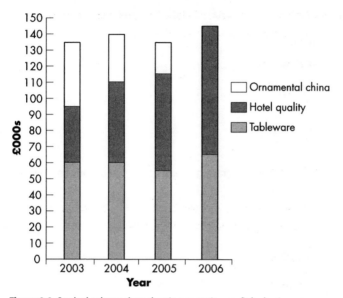

Figure 2.8 Stacked column chart showing operating profit by business type

11 In 2006 no ornamental china was produced. How much extra profit did hotel quality make in this year compared with the previous year.

   a £60,000

   b £20,000

   c £55,000

   d £65,000

   e £80,000

12 What was the total operating profit in 2004?

   a £120,000

   b £130,000

   c £135,000

   d £140,000

   e £145,000

13 How much operating profit was made on ornamental china in 2003?

   a £50,000

   b £60,000

   c £40,000

   d £135,000

   e £35,000

14 Which year was the most profitable for the department producing hotel quality china?

   a 2003

   b 2004

   c 2005

   d 2006

   e Cannot tell

15 What was the total operating profit made over the four years by the ornamental china department?

a £90,000

b £80,000

c £70,000

d £60,000

e £50,000

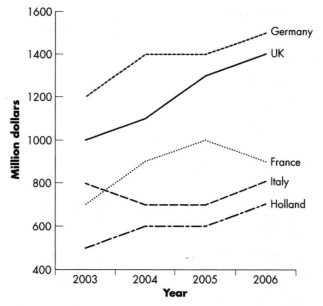

Figure 2.9 Line diagram showing amount spent on computer imports

Answer the following five questions using information contained in the line diagram in Figure 2.9.

16 In 2005, how much more than Italy did Germany spend on computer imports?

a $650 million

b $700 million

c $750 million

d $800 million

e $850 million

17 If the amount spent on computer imports into the United Kingdom in 2007 was 20% lower than in 2006, what was spent in 2007?

a $1080 million

b $1120 million

c $1160 million

d $1220 million

e $1300 million

18 Which countries experienced a drop in the value of computers imported from one year to the next?

a France and Italy

b France and Holland

c Holland and Italy

d UK and Holland

e Italy and UK

19 In 2006, how much less than the United Kingdom did France spend on computer imports?

   a $400 million

   b $700 million

   c $500 million

   d $1400 million

   e $900 million

20 By how much did the amount spent by Italy decrease between 2003 and 2004?

   a 0

   b $800 million

   c $10 million

   d $700 million

   e $100 million

TEST 10

MIXED TEST

(Answers to this test can be found on pages 183–186.)

Finally, here's a test that contains a mixture of the various types of questions.

Allow yourself 20 minutes.

Answer the first 10 questions in this test without using a calculator.

1 329 + 75 = ?

2 12745 − 8329 = ?

3 535 × 11 = ?

4 396 ÷ 6 = ?

The following questions have a choice of five answers – select the one you think is correct.

5 If you have savings of £12,500 then spend £8955 on a new car, how much will you have left?

a £3555

b £3545

c £3455

d £4355

e £3535

6 If you buy six cans of beans at 25p each and a loaf at 95p, how much will you have spent?

a £2.95

b £2.25

c £1.95

d £3.25

e £2.45

7 If a box of 100 pens costs £12, how much is that per pen?

a 20p

b 15p

c 12p

d 10p

e £1.20

8 If you buy a new sofa priced at £550 but negotiate yourself a 10% discount, how much will you pay for the sofa?

a £495

b £500

c £605

d £450

e £505

For the next two questions in this test, you must estimate the answers. Note the word ESTIMATE. For each question you are required to choose the answer, from the five answers given, which is nearest to your estimate.

9 96 + 111 + 1056 =

a 1310

b 1200

c 2150

d 1350

e 1250

10 A third of 9876

a 2950

b 3700

c 3000

d 3300

e 3500

Solve the following problems using a calculator if you wish. There is a choice of five answers given. Only one of these answers is correct.

11 Two ninths of 405?

  a 60

  b 45

  c 90

  d 81

  e 18

12 0.75 as a fraction?

  a $\frac{4}{7}$

  b $\frac{7}{10}$

  c $\frac{2}{3}$

  d $\frac{1}{2}$

  e $\frac{3}{4}$

13 35% of 600?

  a 210

  b 350

  c 195

  d 200

  e 330

14 A company has 220 employees, 25% of which are women. How many male employees are there?

  a 55

  b 110

  c 170

  d 165

  e 60

15 $\frac{3}{100}$ as a decimal?

  a 0.003

  b 0.03

  c 0.3

  d 0.01

  e 0.1

In this next group of five questions, find the missing number indicated by a question mark.

16 85, 82, 76, 67, 55, ?

  a 43

  b 52

  c 50

  d 45

  e 40

17 19, 24, ?, 34, 39, 44

  a 26

  b 29

  c 31

  d 30

  e 28

18 23, 46, 92, ?, 368, 736

  a 184

  b 342

  c 200

  d 180

  e 176

19 76, 79, 84, 91, 100, 111, ?

  a 98

  b 126

  c 130

  d 115

  e 124

20 105, 99, 93, ?, 81, 75

  a 85

  b 89

  c 87

  d 79

  e 90

The final five questions in this mixed test use information from Table 2.4.

Table 2.4 Middlechester Chamber of Commerce employers' survey results

Type of business	Average no. of employees	No. of businesses in category
Manufacturing	43	27
Catering	15	11
Call centres	65	2
Retail	8	28
Local authority	253	1

21 Approximately how many people were employed in the catering industry in Middlechester?

  a 15

  b 190

  c 165

  d 11

  e 65

22 How many businesses in total took part in the survey?

  a 27

  b 67

  c 87

  d 69

  e 79

23 How many people in total worked in either a call centre or for the local authority?

  a 393

  b 318

  c 253

  d 385

  e 383

24 Which type of business employed the greatest number of employees?

  a Manufacturing

  b Catering

  c Call centres

  d Retail

  e Local authority

25 How many people were employed by the businesses that took part in the survey?

a 1955

b 1933

c 2033

d 384

e 1845

CHAPTER THREE
ANSWERS TO AND
EXPLANATIONS OF TIMED TESTS

TEST 1

ARITHMETIC

This first test is a mixture of questions testing your knowledge of the four basic rules of arithmetic – addition, subtraction, multiplication and division. It is this type of question where practice should really help you.

If you find that you are struggling with basic arithmetic tests, ask yourself whether it is because of the time constraints or because you have difficulty using the four basic rules. If you feel that the problem is that you are too tense or that you panic because you are working against the clock, go to Chapter 4. Look at the relaxation techniques and advice, then put some into practice. If, however, you think that you need a better understanding of arithmetic, get some help. Go back to basics by finding a course – enquire at your local college – or buy yourself a book. You might also benefit from some individual tuition in basic arithmetic.

1 125

2 87

3 23

4 20

5 72

6 100

7 37

8 81

9 195

10 9

Questions 1 to 10 – Unless you have got all these questions correct, you would benefit from more practice and also from a little revision of the basic concepts. Know your multiplication tables and try to visualise the addition and subtraction problems. If you can picture putting the figures to be added together one under the other – just as you would do if you were writing the sum down on paper – it might help to avoid mistakes and you might see the solution a little quicker.

Practise, practise, practise!

For the next ten questions, there is a different method of giving the answer. These are multiple-choice questions so you will need to follow instructions to the letter. Take great care that you understand how you are to indicate your answer. Some multiple-choice papers will ask you to circle the correct answer while others will ask you to indicate with a tick or a cross. Another popular method is to instruct you to indicate your choice by shading in a circle or pair of brackets (similar to how you would fill in your lottery numbers) on a separate answer paper. This paper will then be read, using a template, by the person marking the tests.

It is important that you do not assume what is required of you – be sure to read the instructions carefully.

The answers to multiple-choice questions frequently contain very similar choices, so extra care must be taken. In haste you may choose the wrong answer from the possibilities even though you have worked out the correct answer for yourself. The solution to this is to jot down your answer as you work and then choose from the selections given. You may also notice that misleading answers are sometimes given – transposing figures giving answers of 23 and 32 to choose from, for example, or there may be answers that cater for common mistakes, such as adding rather than subtracting.

Decimals are easy to deal with provided that you remember to keep the decimal point in the right place. With addition and subtraction this is simple – just keep the figures lined up neatly under one another and the decimal point will stay in the correct place. More people have problems with this when they are multiplying or dividing. Here, it will pay to practise estimating what your answer should be. If you have to multiply 45.9 by 1.9, for example, the answer should be close to 90.0 – not 900.0 or 9.0 which might be the answer you come up with if you let the decimal point wander to the right or left of where it belongs. Having done this timed test, run through the explanations for these questions below.

11 Answer **c** 99.0 is correct. Here you might find it useful to estimate or round up part of the question. If you round up 19.8 to 20, it will then be much easier for you to see that the answer must be slightly less than 100. You will then be able to rule out all the other answers fairly quickly.

12 Answer **a** 184 is correct. Here scanning the answers may be useful. You know that the answer must be over 160 and will end in 4 as, splitting the sum into more manageable parts, 8 × 20 is 160 and 8 × 3 is 24. Only one answer again will be possible and you might find it without doing the whole calculation.

13 Answer **b** 23.5 is correct. Do not let the decimal point throw you off balance – this is a simple addition and there are no answers put in here to confuse. The question and the answers are straightforward.

14 Answer **e** 116 is correct – again a simple addition. The thing to watch out for here is that you do not subtract instead of add – that's what the answer **b** 88 is there for. You just might have chosen the wrong answer in your haste.

15 Answer **e** 15.5 is correct. A simple subtraction involving decimals.

16 Answer **b** 204 is correct. Another addition but there are a couple of answers also ending in 4 that will have been put in there to confuse. This highlights the need to work accurately.

17 Answer **a** 94 is correct. A simple subtraction but do not make the mistake of adding rather than subtracting.

18 Answer **d** 32 is correct. The first of the division calculations in this section – it is an easy one to start you off.

19 Answer **b** 29.1 is correct. Jot your answer down as you work through the question from right to left so that you do not transpose the figures by mistake.

20 Answer **a** 25 is correct. Another simple division.

The next ten questions deal mainly with money amounts but they still test your ability with the four basic rules – addition, subtraction, multiplication and division. They also incorporate the decimal point so remember to keep it in the right place. Again these are multiple-choice questions and a facility for knowing the approximate answer you are looking for will be useful here.

21 Answer **b** £19.95 is correct. Rounding up is the easiest way to go about this question. If one ream of paper were to cost £4.00, then 5 × 4 is simple. This rules out a couple of the suggested answers straight away and, with care, you will quickly get the right answer.

22 Answer **e** £309.97 is correct. The safest route to the correct answer is by jotting down and adding up all the amounts in the question.

23 Answer **c** £120,000 is correct. This is a simple calculation involving an average, that is, finding the total by multiplying the number of people involved by the average for the group.

24 Answer **e** 40.0 is correct. This is working with time. First you need to calculate the number of hours per day – allowing for the half hour for lunch – 8 hours per day. Then simply multiply by 5 to get the weekly total.

25 Answer **d** £510,000 is correct. This is a simple multiplication but you must be careful that you get the right number of zeros in your answer. Two of the incorrect answers are included in your choices specifically to penalise carelessness in this area.

26 Answer **a** £11,035 is correct. Take the two amounts – the deductions from the pay – away from the gross pay – to arrive at the net pay.

27 Answer **a** £75.00 is correct. Simply divide the total money available for the bonuses by the number of people to arrive at the share for one person.

28 Answer **c** £46,000 is correct. This is a straightforward subtraction – just make sure to keep the zeros in the right place and take care to subtract and not add by mistake.

29 Answer **e** 37.5 is correct. Multiply the number of people by the amount of overtime, i.e. 15 × 2.5.

30 Answer **c** £76,500 is correct. This is the first time that a percentage has come into these tests. Do not panic! Percentages are just another, more simple, way of stating a part of a whole. Percentages are very similar to fractions and ten per cent is the same as one tenth. So finding ten per cent is the same as finding a tenth – you just have to divide by ten. When you have found the ten per cent, do not forget to subtract that ten per cent from the whole as the ten per cent represents a discount, i.e. 85,000 ÷ 10 = 8,500, then 85,000 − 8,500 = 76,500.

31 Answer **c** 5.1 is correct. A simple addition involving two numbers, both of which have decimal points so care must be taken here.

32 Answer **e** 38 is correct. Three numbers to add together here. Several of the answers are at about the right level so do not be tempted to guess.

33 Answer **a** 42 is correct. A simple subtraction but one of the answers would be correct if the question required addition so be careful not to fall into that trap.

34 Answer **e** 138.8 is correct. Another subtraction question but this time with two figures using decimal points. Take care.

35 Answer **b** 1815 is correct. As this is a multiple choice question, one way to tackle this would be to estimate your answer. 242 multiplied by 10 is 2420, multiplied by 5 is 1210, so the answer must be midway between these two figures.

36 Answer **e** 1767.12 is correct. Large numbers combined with decimal points in both the figures in the question can be difficult to deal with so be sure to work out the answer carefully on rough paper.

37 Answer **a** 1215 is correct. This division question might be worth calculating in your head as it involves dividing by five. Most people are comfortable with multiplying and dividing by five or ten. If you are in any doubt, jot it down.

38 Answer **b** 2010 is correct. This one involves large numbers and all the answer choices are similar. This can be very confusing, especially when you are under extra pressure from the test situation and trying to work as quickly as possible. Remember the advice that accuracy is usually more important than speed.

39 Answer **d** 2560 is correct. Again the answer choices are similar and can disorientate you. Continue to work methodically and use the calculator if you are in any doubt at all about your answer.

40 Answer **e** 606.17 is correct. A quick glance at this question should tell you that the answer will be in the region of 600 – by subtracting 200 from 800. Only two answers meet this requirement and only one of these has a decimal point – so select that one. This demonstrates the value of developing a facility to immediately assess an approximate answer, and only extensive practice will help you with this.

TEST 2

PERCENTAGES, FRACTIONS AND SEQUENCES

Calculations involving percentages and fractions can cause panic in many people – especially under test conditions and time constraints. However, it must be remembered that we use percentages and fractions every day. We are all familiar with interest rates shown in newspapers and fractions used in shops – the offer of half price goods for example.

What we sometimes fail to appreciate is that percentages and fractions are closely connected. Percentages are, in fact, fractions expressed as parts of one hundred. This helps us with comparison of increases or decreases by using a common standard – the one part in a hundred method, that is, one per cent of a quantity is one hundredth of it.

With this in mind, we can tackle the explanations for this test.

1 Answer **a** 100 is correct. Remembering that one per cent is one in a hundred, twenty in a hundred – 20% – could also be expressed as $\frac{20}{100}$. It is then easy to see that this is the same as one fifth, so divide 500 by 5 to get one fifth – 100 is the answer.

2 Answer **c** 90 is correct. Again using the one part in one hundred rule, we can see that 45% is 45 in 100. So in two hundred, 45 is multiplied by two to give 90.

3 Answer **e** 0.20 is correct. This question combines fractions and decimals – but do not let that put you off. Decimals, as the name suggests, simply express tenths of a number. Accordingly, one fifth could also be expressed (albeit rather clumsily) as two tenths, which would be 0.2 expressed decimally.

4 Answer **a** $\frac{9}{10}$ is correct. This is similar to the previous question – but in reverse. You are asked to express a decimal as a fraction. As explained before, 0.1 is equivalent to $\frac{1}{10}$ so 0.9 will obviously be nine tenths.

5 Answer **e** 2 is correct. This question introduces simple algebra and again this is something that frequently scares people who are not confident about their numerical ability. However, basic algebra merely substitutes symbols (letters) for the numbers that we are trying to find to solve the equation. In this question we are trying to discover the number represented by x so we need to ask ourselves what number, multiplied by 5 (as in the expression 5x) would give us 10? A simple question for you at this stage, x = 2.

6 Answer **b** 3 is correct. Basic algebra again. First deal with the 7. If this is to be deducted from the left side of the equation, it must also be deducted from the other. $37 - 7 = 30$ so now we have $10x = 30$. Following the method in the previous question, it is easy to see that $x = 3$ in this question.

7 Answer **d** 60 is correct. Back to fractions here. It might help you to restate the question as '10 is a sixth of what?' We can see then that 60 (six times ten) is the answer.

8 Answer **a** 4.5 is correct. Here you need to understand decimals. You will recall that decimals deal with tenth parts of a whole number so this question tests your understanding of decimals. It asks, in effect, 'do you know where to place the decimal point?' Since you are trying to find one tenth, the decimal point must move just one place to the left – $\frac{1}{10}$ of 45 is therefore 4.5.

9 Answer **b** 19 is correct. With a fraction of one eighth, you simply need to divide the whole number by eight and you will arrive at the correct answer representing one of eight parts of the whole.

10 Answer **b** 12 is correct. Back to percentages and you will need to divide the number by 100 to get one per cent and then multiply your answer by 15 to get 15%, i.e. $80 \div 100 = 0.8$, $0.8 \times 15 = 12$. Alternatively you could just use the percentage function on your calculator. It is useful, though, to try doing this type of calculation both ways to ensure that you understand what you are doing and to get a feel for the answer to expect.

In the next ten questions you are being asked to perform similar calculations to the previous ten. The difference is that this time they are disguised with words. You must translate the word problems – in your head, and quickly – into the simple calculations that they represent. If you go through these explanations – even if you have done well on this section – you will notice the connection between percentages and fractions.

11 The answer is 56. All you have to do here is divide the total number of people who applied by four, i.e. $224 \div 4 = 56$.

12 The answer is 132. To find 20 per cent of the figure you have to divide by 5, i.e. $660 \div 5 = 132$.

13 The answer is 25%. This is the same type of question as the first two but it is asked the other way round. The question could be restated as $64 \div 16 = 4$ and you should know that a quarter (one fourth) is equivalent to 25%.

14 The answer is £231.00. This is a little more involved but uses the same principles. The first part of your calculation should be £220 $\div$ 100 $\times$ 5 (or £2.20 – if you move the decimal point two places to the left – $\times$ 5) = £11.00 then £220 + £11.00 = £231.00. Do not forget, having found the five per cent, to add it back on to the original figure to get the new figure including the 5% increase.

15 The answer is 10%. Here, by restating nine out of ten as $\frac{9}{10}$, you can see quite clearly the link between fractions and percentages. $\frac{9}{10}$ is 90% so the remainder is $\frac{1}{10}$ or 10%.

16 The answer is 5%. In this question you must first work out £4.00 + ? = £4.20 or, put another way, £4.20 − £4.00 = £0.20, then calculate what percentage of £4.00 is £0.20. Remembering that a percentage is a fraction of one hundred, you need to express the 20 pence as parts of 100. Hence, $20 \times 100 \div 400 = 5$.

17 The answer is 80. Despite there being 100 involved in this question, you are not required to work with percentages! This is a simple fraction so divide the number of workers by five to get the number who have received training, but remember that you are asked to find the number who have not been trained so subtract your answer, from the original number to get your answer, i.e. $100 \div 5 = 20$ then $100 - 20 = 80$.

18 The answer is £160. Do not let the mention of an average throw you off course – this question merely asks you to state half of the total, i.e. $£320 \div 2 = £160$.

19 The answer is 306. Work out one quarter then multiply it by three to get three quarters, i.e. $(408 \div 4) \times 3 = 306$. This is the same as if you had taken the 102 ($\frac{1}{4}$) away from the total.

20 The answer is 82. This is similar to the last question, i.e. $(123 \div 3) \times 2 = 82$.

Number sequences form the next group of questions. Being successful with number sequence questions is dependent on your being able to spot the pattern in the numbers. As always, speed and accuracy are important. However, if you spend a little time now on your practice and on working through the explanations, you will soon see how the patterns develop and become quicker at completing this type of test. There are some number sequences that come up time and time again and it will benefit you to become familiar with these. Useful patterns include square roots (the square root of 16 is 4 for example), squared numbers (4 squared is 16, 3 squared is 9 and so on), basic multiplication tables and prime numbers (numbers that can only be divided by 1 and by themselves, i.e. 2, 3, 5, 7, 11, 13 and so on). Unless the pattern is immediately apparent to you, your first move when faced with a number sequence question should be to work out (and note down) the difference between each pair of figures. This will often give you the answer straight away if you can see a pattern in the differences you have noted down.

21 Answer **d** 50 is correct. Here an odd number, increasing each time, is added to the previous number so the sequence can be solved as follows: 2 (+3), 5 (+5), 10 (+7), 17 (+9), 26 (+11), 37 (+13) = 50. As you can see, there is a pattern within a pattern here – the numbers added each time are 3, 5, 7, 9, 11 so the final one to be added must be 13.

22 Answer **b** 20 is correct. Work out the difference between each pair of numbers and you will see that 7 has been added to the preceding number in each case. The missing number in this question is in the middle of the sequence whereas often it will be at the end. This can appear to be more difficult but the same principles apply – look for the pattern.

23 Answer **e** 729 is correct. Here the numbers rise rapidly and this should alert you to a possible multiplying factor. As you will see, each number has been multiplied by three.

24 Answer **b** 32 is correct. This is a common sequence – each number has been doubled.

25 Answer **c** 45 is correct. The decreasing pattern here should be obvious – the numbers decrease by 10 each time.

26 Answer **e** 27 is correct. The quickest way to spot this sequence is to jot down the difference between each pair of numbers. 3 is added then 4 then 5 and so on until the end when you will know that you should add 7.

27 Answer **a** 64 is correct. This is one of the common sequences referred to above. The sequence is $3 \times 3 = 9$, $4 \times 4 = 16, 5 \times 5 = 25, 6 \times 6 = 36, 7 \times 7 = 49$ so the next one must be $8 \times 8 = 64$.

28 Answer **c** 80 is correct. There is a decrease of 4 between each pair of numbers.

29 Answer **b** 49 is correct. For this question you need to spot the pattern by working out the difference between each pair of numbers, i.e. 3, 6, 9 and so on.

30 Answer **b** 46 is correct. Here is another decreasing pattern but this time it alternates between 5 and 10. The next decrease in the sequence should be 5.

The next ten questions are about error location and you will find that the questions here are similar to the number sequence ones. The way in which you go about solving this type of question is also very similar – you need to spot the pattern. However, many candidates have been known to panic when faced with error location questions. Keep calm, work methodically and you will be able to see the error in the sequence. When you find the right answer, the sequence runs perfectly. You are looking for the 'odd one out', the number in the sequence that does not belong. Its presence spoils the pattern.

31 Answer **d** 12 is correct. A quick glance here should tell you that the number 12 looks out of place – it is the only even number in this sequence. A check of the difference between each pair of numbers shows you that, with the exception of the numbers on either side of the 12, 2 is added to each number. Therefore, if you add 2 to 11 and substitute 13 for the 12, you will have continued the sequence correctly and it now runs perfectly.

32 Answer **c** 80 is correct. Here, the answer is perhaps not quite so obvious so you should immediately perform the first stage in your process to find the answer – note down the difference between each pair of numbers. You will see that 5 has been added, then 10, then 15 – so far so good – but then the sequence goes awry when 15 is added again. You should then try continuing the sequence that you had started – add 5, then 10, then 15, then 20. As that works and makes the sequence make sense, you have found the error.

33 Answer **a** 11 is correct. The error in this sequence is at the beginning of the question, so that can make things a little more confusing. Do not let this deter you, just continue to the end of the sequence, noting the difference between each pair of figures. At the end the pattern becomes obvious – you need to deduct 2 each time. With a decreasing sequence like this it can often help to read the sequence backwards. If you had read 2, 4, 6, 8, you may have easily spotted the error as this is a sequence that is very familiar to all of us.

34 Answer **e** 17 is correct. Here 6 is added between each pair of numbers so that the 17 should be 18 to follow this pattern.

35 Answer **a** 50 is correct. Fifteen is subtracted between each pair of numbers.

36 Answer **b** 123 is correct. Seven is subtracted between each pair of numbers.

37 Answer **a** 8375 is correct. Here each number is multiplied by 5 and this is easy to spot in the earlier numbers in the sequence, which are smaller and therefore more manageable. The last figure in the sequence should be 9375.

38 Answer **e** 40 is correct. Each figure is double the preceding one.

39 Answer **b** 25 is correct. The odd one out here is the one that it is not possible to divide by 3. A quick way to check if a number is divisible by 3, is to add up the digits in the number and see if that is divisible by 3, e.g. 81 = 8+1 = 9 and 9 is a multiple of 3. If a consistently decreasing or increasing pattern is not present – as in this case – then you must look for something that all the numbers have in common.

40 Answer **b** 12 is correct. Check the differences between each pair of numbers. They increase by 1 then 2 then 3 and so on making 12 the odd one out.

TEST 3

INFORMATION FROM CHARTS AND TABLES

In Table 2.1 you need to notice – and remember! – that the figures shown against each type of training are percentages. You will therefore frequently need to calculate the actual number using the percentage figure and the total number of staff in that year, that is, do not simply quote the percentage figure unless that is specifically asked for. Unless you are specifically told not to write on the question paper, it is a good idea to jot down any calculations like this that you have to make – they may come in useful later.

1 Answer **e** 18 is correct. In 2006, 6% of the total number of staff received managerial training so the calculation is as follows: 1% of 300 = 3, 3 × 6 = 18. Note the easy way to calculate one per cent – by dividing by one hundred; then multiply by six to get your answer.

2 Answer **a** 17 is correct. The questions in this section are changing from simply reading off a figure from the table to having to work out a percentage and then back again, so take care to read the question carefully. Make sure that you know what is being asked for. Here, you need to compare actual numbers of staff receiving a particular type of training in a specific year so you will need to calculate the numbers first.

3 Answer **c** 50 is correct. Here you are simply required to read the numbers from the table – rather than working out percentages – and subtract one from the other.

4 Answer **e** 40 is correct. Again simply read from the table.

5 Answer **b** 120 is correct. First you need to pinpoint the correct year – 2006 – then work out the appropriate percentage of staff, i.e. 40% of 300 = 120.

The next five questions use information presented in a pie chart. Pie charts are often used to show data expressed as percentages, and the questions associated with this type of chart will usually involve your having to calculate percentages of a total figure in addition to reading off and comparing information from the charts.

6 Answer **c** 7% is correct. In this question – a straightforward one to start with – you are asked to compare a percentage figure from one year with the corresponding figure from the other year, that is, simply reading off the percentages stated for the 'will increase orders' section in each year. Take care to read the question so that you do not waste time calculating the difference in terms of actual numbers of customers rather than just the percentage.

7 Answer **c** 45 is correct. In contrast to the previous question, you are asked here for the number of customers responding in a certain way (rather than just the percentage). You will therefore have to use the information provided to work out the number of customers, i.e. work out 15% of 300.

8 Answer **a** 33 is correct. Here you are comparing the number of customers in a particular category in one year with the number in the same category in another year, i.e. calculate 34% of 300 (2005), then 45% of 300 (2006), then take one from the other to arrive at your answer. An easy way to do this is to say 34% of 100 is 34 then multiply by 3. It may be useful to jot down the answers on the relevant area of the chart whenever you calculate percentages like this – you will then not need to repeat the calculation if you have to use it in another question.

9 Answer **b** 78 is correct. Again you are dealing with actual numbers so you must do the calculations. Take care to use the figures from the right year.

10 Answer **d** 129 is correct. Another simple calculation after you have worked out the numbers involved. The calculation would therefore be $(45 \times 3) - (2 \times 3) = 135 - 6 = 129$.

The next five questions are based on a column chart. This sort of chart needs to be read carefully. Pay particular attention to the key (also known as the legend) and the axes labels – in this example they will tell you that the profit shown on the chart represents thousands of pounds and the use of shading in the columns shows how to differentiate the various profit centres. Almost always some of the answers will be misleading. For example, they may be given – incorrectly – in the same amount as shown in the columns rather than in thousands of pounds and, because you will be dealing with large figures, there may be a choice of answers given that look correct – apart from the addition of one very important zero!

11 Answer **b** £200,000 is correct. First you must locate the year in which most profit was made – 2005 – then simply read off the value of profit made by the children's section, remembering that the answer will be in £000s. Do not fall into the trap!

12 Answer **a** 25% is correct. Proportions may be given in percentages or fractions. Here the answer is expressed as a percentage. Again you need to find the relevant year – 2002 – then read off the answer. You will note that the exact answer would be a little over £200,000. However, the question calls for a rough proportion so you will need to approximate.

13 Answer **e** £800,000 is correct. Here you will need to go along the five columns relating to children's clothes and add up the amounts shown. Again, remember that the answer will be in thousands of pounds.

14 Answer **a** Women's is correct. There is only one year in which Workwear made less than £500,000 operating profit – 2002. Read the question carefully and note that you are required to state the second most profitable area, not the most profitable.

15 Answer **a** £1,100,000 is correct. Here you need to pay particular attention to the number of zeros – some of the answer choices are quite confusing so you must be clear about the number you are looking for amongst the choices. In the year 2004 (the third most profitable year) you can see that the total profit column ends at a point midway between 1000 and 1200 in the chart. This represents £1,100,000 – not £1100 or £11,100,000!

Another type of chart is used for the next five questions in this test – a line diagram. These are used to display trends and to compare similar figures from different sources. You must read figures from the graph to get the information for your answers.

As with all graphs and charts, you must take care that you note the information in the key.

16 Answer **d** Company D is correct. Company D starts at the lowest point of all the companies at £20,000 in 2002 and finishes in 2005 as the highest of all the companies that year. You should therefore be able to see the answer to this question at a glance.

17 Answer **a** £510,000 is correct. This is simply a matter of reading off and adding together the values for all four companies in 2006. Take care that you add in two turnovers of £140,000 where Companies B and D are at the same point.

18 Answer **e** £120,000 is correct. First you need to look for the company whose line on the diagram does not dip at all (Company D) – if the line dips, of course, it denotes a fall in the value on that axis. Read off its turnover figures in 2002 and 2006. Deduct the 2002 figure from the figure for 2006 to get your answer.

19 Answer **c** £20,000 is correct. In 2003 Company A's turnover was £70,000 and Company B's was £90,000. Subtraction will give you the correct answer.

20 Answer **c** Company C is correct. The turnover of two companies – Company A and Company B – fell by £30,000 each and Company D's turnover rose by £40,000, while Company C's turnover fell by £40,000 – the biggest fall.

TEST 4

ARITHMETIC

Questions 1 to 10 – If you get any of these questions wrong, it might be useful to look back at the advice in the section of this chapter for Test 1.

1 73.2

2 8.0

3 375

4 2.25

5 41

6 32.4

7 11.89

8 231.1

9 46.9

10 42.8

The answers are quite straightforward – there are no tricks or traps. Practice is the most effective way to improve your scores in this type of question. Here again you are being tested on your command of the four important arithmetical operations. Your accuracy is also being evaluated and many of the answers are similar or are put there specifically to confuse – so take care.

Now the multiple choice questions.

11 Answer **e** 891 is correct. If you estimate this answer by rounding up 297 to 300, then you will know that the answer to look for is slightly less than 900.

12 Answer **b** 60.1 is correct. Do not rush this one – many of the answers are very close.

13 Answer **a** 9.7 is correct. A simple division – you do not even need to worry too much about the decimal point as none of the answers use this to confuse you.

14 Answer **c** 14 is correct. Another simple division that you should be able to do in your head. If not, practise this type of mental arithmetic while shopping or paying bills.

15 Answer **b** 321 is correct. Work this out in two parts, i.e. 3 × 100 and 3 × 7, if it makes it easier for you.

16 Answer **b** 148 is correct. This should be easier if you start the addition from the right-hand side and note down your answer – but be careful, several of the answers are very similar.

17 Answer **d** 115 is correct. An easy sum, but take care – one of the answers is there to fool you if you mistakenly add instead of subtract.

18 Answer **a** 11.18 is correct. The only difficulty here might be the decimal point so accuracy in your choice from the available answers is important – they all look quite similar.

19 Answer **e** 284 is correct. Perhaps an easy way to work this out is to move the decimal point to multiply by 10 then double it to get your answer.

20 Answer **c** 71 is correct. A simple subtraction but maybe you would find it easier to round up the 297 to 300?

21 Answer **b** £15.50 is correct. Do not waste time here. If you understand that the average is the same as equal shares, then you will not need to work out the total bill and divide by the number of people to get the amount that represents an equal share – you have already been told the answer!

22 Answer **e** £52.25 is correct. Work out ten per cent of the bill (by moving the decimal point to the left) and then do not forget to add it to the bill to find out the total amount to pay, including the ten per cent tip.

23 Answer **a** 693 mm is correct. Again you are being asked to work out ten per cent and then add it on to the original amount. This illustrates the value of being able to 'see' immediately what 10 per cent of an amount is and the same could be said of being able to calculate 5 per cent easily (find 10 per cent by moving the decimal point one place to the left, then simply divide this by 2) or 1 per cent (move the decimal point two places to the left) or twenty per cent (find ten per cent and double it) – practice will help this to become second nature to you. Do not forget to add the two amounts together.

24 Answer **b** 3 hours 10 minutes is correct. Here you need to find the number of pages to be printed, then divide by the number of pages per minute. Finally convert this to hours and minutes, i.e. $10 \times 76 \div 4 = 190$ minutes $= 3$ hours 10 minutes. Several of the answers are given in just minutes – do not be fooled into using one of these. The question asks for an answer given in hours and minutes so make sure you ignore any answer that does not comply with this instruction.

25 Answer **b** 39.1p is correct. Using a calculator this is a simple division, i.e. £3519.00 ÷ 9000 = 39.1. The only aspect that needs extra care is that you get the decimal point in the correct place and you will see that several of the answers are similar except for the decimal point (3.91p, £0.39 and the correct answer 39.1p).

26 Answer **e** £2805.00 is correct. Your calculation should be (200 × £16.50) − 15% = £2805.00.

27 Answer **c** 6 hours is correct. One worker would take four times as long to do the job as four workers so multiply $1\frac{1}{2}$ by 4 to get the correct answer of 6 hours.

28 Answer **a** £1655.00 is correct. This question demands that you are very careful with the decimal point. All the answers use the same figures with just the decimal point and number of 5s determining the right figure.

29 Answer **d** £3200 is correct. Here you should multiply 80p by 4 then move the decimal point three places to the right to multiply by 1000.

30 Answer **d** 118 is correct. An easy subtraction 127 − 9.

31 Answer **b** 26 is correct. A simple subtraction followed by an addition. Try again with your calculator if you got this one wrong.

32 Answer **e** 1.67 is correct. These are only small numbers but it can be useful to use a calculator for this type of question – but make sure that it will give the answer correct to two decimal places.

33 Answer **d** 249.1 is correct. Again, a straightforward question but several of the answers are similar so you could get confused if you rush.

34 Answer **a** 599.2 is correct. Your calculator may give you the answer 599.1666 recurring (i.e. the six going on ad infinitum) but that answer is not included in the choice, so you should choose the nearest one. As is usual, the choices will use a maximum of two decimal places.

35 Answer **b** 3977 is correct. A straightforward multiplication – easy to do with a calculator.

36 Answer **a** 110 is correct. Take care that you do the arithmetical operations in the correct order.

37 Answer **c** 901.22 is correct. All the answers are similar so take care that you read your answer off the calculator correctly.

38 Answer **b** 2250 is correct. Again, similar answers – this tests not just your ability to use your calculator but also your accuracy under pressure.

39 Answer **b** 663.2 is correct. Confusing figures so take care.

40 Answer **e** 4243 is correct. Accuracy is the key.

TEST 5

PERCENTAGES, FRACTIONS AND SEQUENCES

The key to solving questions where fractions are to be expressed as percentages, and vice versa, is to remember that percentages are just another kind of fraction. They are fractions of one hundred.

1 Answer **c** £3.50 is correct. To work out this percentage, divide by 100 then multiply by 17.5, i.e. 19.99 ÷ 100 = .1999 × 17.5 = £3.50. An alternative way would be to work out 10% then 5% (by halving 10%) then 2.5% (by halving 5%) then add all three figures together to get 17.5%.

2 Answer **b** £9.40 is correct. Remembering that 25% is the same as $\frac{1}{4}$, this question is relatively easy – simply divide £37.60 by 4.

3 Answer **c** 50 is correct. $12\frac{1}{2}$% can also be expressed as $\frac{1}{8}$ or half of 25%, so use whichever of these ways of looking at the question seems easiest to you. With a multiple-choice question you should try to get an immediate idea of the approximate answer. It is often the case that there is only one possible answer, that is, the one that comes close to what you have estimated.

4 Answer **b** 950 is correct. This question will show your ability to work with larger numbers and to keep the right number of zeros in the answer. 95% of 100 is obviously 95, so 95% of 1000 must have one zero added, i.e. 950.

5 Answer **d** 11.1 is correct. This is simple but you will need to take care that you keep the decimal point in the right place.

6 Answer **b** £40 is correct. Understanding that 100% of £10 is £10, will show you that 400% must simply be four times the original amount.

7 Answer **d** $\frac{1}{5}$ is correct. 0.2 can be expressed as $\frac{2}{10}$. However, this is not the lowest form of this fraction so you would reduce it to its correct expression of $\frac{1}{5}$.

8 Answer **a** 150 is correct. This is easy if you have a basic understanding of fractions – essential if you want to pass tests of this type – simply divide 450 by 3. However, if you have problems, get help with fractions.

9 Answer **e** $9\frac{1}{2}$ is correct. Finding the common denominator (the number at the bottom of the fraction that can be common to both parts of this sum) is the key to this question. In this case it is 6 so the calculation is as follows: $10\frac{4}{6} - 1\frac{1}{6} = 9\frac{3}{6} = 9\frac{1}{2}$.

10 Answer **d** $37\frac{1}{4}$ is correct. Here again this is straightforward – the common denominator is 4, i.e. $15\frac{2}{4} + 21\frac{3}{4} = 37\frac{1}{4}$.

11 Answer **c** 4% is correct. How many times does 25 divide into 100? Four is the answer when $\frac{1}{25}$ is expressed as a percentage.

12 Answer **d** $\frac{9}{20}$ is correct. This is a similar calculation to the previous question – but the other way round. Expressed as a fraction, 45% is forty-five one hundredths – but take care, the question asks for it to be expressed in its simplest form so you will need to reduce the fraction as far as you can by dividing the numerator (the number at the top of the fraction) and the denominator (the number at the bottom) by the same number – in this case 5.

13 Answer **a** $\frac{11}{16}$ is correct. Here you must find the common denominator – 16 – then add the numerators, multiplying the 3 in $\frac{3}{8}$ to ensure that it is expressed as 16ths so $\frac{6}{16}$ + $\frac{5}{16} = \frac{11}{16}$.

14 Answer **d** $\frac{5}{6}$ is correct. With a common denominator of 6, it is easy to see that the numerator is 5.

15 Answer **b** 40% is correct. The calculation here could be expressed as $(100 \div 5) \times 2 = 40$.

16 Answer **a** £47.25 is correct. A quick way to work this out is to see that 10% is £4.50 and half of that would be the 5% that you are looking for, i.e. £2.25 – and do not forget to add the £45.00 to get your answer.

17 Answer **d** 70 is correct. Here you just need to divide 210 by 3 to find a third.

18 Answer **b** 100 is correct. This is a test of your skill in extracting the relevant facts from the question. The subject of the survey is not important. Summed up, the question tells you that 75% responded and therefore 25% did not. 25% of 400 is easy to work out – simply divide by 4.

19 Answer **e** £300,000 is correct. The calculation here is $\frac{1}{2} + \frac{1}{3} = \frac{3}{6} + \frac{2}{6} = \frac{5}{6}, \frac{5}{6}$ of £360,000 is £300,000. You could also find a half then a third and add them together.

20 Answer **b** 65% is correct. In this question you need to be careful in organising the relevant information you have been given. 1 in 10 = 10%, add this to the 25% and you have the total percentage who are outside the timespan given, so the remainder $(100 - 35 = 65\%)$ must be what the question requires.

21 Answer **a** 528 is correct. Each time you should subtract 19 from the previous figure. Just work methodically through

the sequence, noting the difference between each pair –
you will then see the pattern. Do not forget to note
whether a subtraction or addition is going on each time.

22 Answer **d** 536 is correct. Twenty-one is added each time
to the preceding number. A quick glance might show you
an obvious pattern such as this, where the last digit in
each number increases each time.

23 Answer **a** 132 is correct. You will see that the numbers
increase as you go through the sequence. Work out the
difference again between each pair of numbers and you
will see that the increase doubles each time, i.e.
differences of 1, 2, 4, 8, 16 – so the next addition should
be 32.

24 Answer **d** 72 is correct. Add 9 each time.

25 Answer **e** 52 is correct. The number is decreasing by 3
more each time, i.e. the change between each pair of
numbers is −3, −6, −9, −12 so the last change should be
−15.

26 Answer **b** 25 is correct. If numbers go down rapidly like
this you should look for a dividing factor – in this case it
is 5.

27 Answer **b** 49 is correct. Add 7 each time.

28 Answer **d** 36 is correct. Starting with 2, the difference
between each pair of numbers increases by 1 each time,
i.e. the sequence between the numbers goes +2, +3, +4,
+5 so add 6 to the last number to get your answer.

29 Answer **a** 729 is correct. If numbers increase rapidly like this you need to look for a multiplying factor. In this case it is 3.

30 Answer **c** 300 is correct. The numbers here decrease by 25 each time. By jotting down the difference between each pair of numbers you will see this pattern and be able to continue it when you see that the difference between the fourth and sixth numbers in the sequence is 50.

31 Answer **c** 34 is correct. Deduct 9 each time. Replace 34 with 36.

32 Answer **b** 128 is correct. The error is at the beginning of the sequence and this can be more difficult to spot. However, if you work methodically through the series, jotting down the difference between each pair of numbers you will see where the pattern is not followed. The sequence alternates between subtracting 23, then adding 21 and the correct number to start this sequence should be 123.

33 Answer **e** 220 is correct. The correct figure – at the end of this sequence – should be 224 as the number doubles each time.

34 Answer **d** 24 is correct. It should have been 28 as the difference between each pair of numbers increases by 2 each time, i.e. +2, +4, +6, +8, +10.

35 Answer **d** 65 is correct. Fifteen is added each time so 70 should have been the number between 55 and 85 in the sequence.

TEST 6

INFORMATION FROM CHARTS AND TABLES

1 Answer **d** 36 is correct. In effect you are being asked to add 20% to the distributors' visitors total, which is 30. Twenty per cent (or one fifth) of 30 is 6. Add together to get the answer, i.e. 30 + 20% = 36.

2 Answer **c** 588 is correct. A simple addition, but one of the answers is misleading – just make sure that you add up the correct column.

3 Answer **b** 72 is correct. Firstly you must find the total number of exhibitors this year (48) then increase by a half, i.e. 48 × 1.5 = 72.

4 Answer **a** Catering is correct. Catering companies logged 188 visitors.

5 Answer **b** Packaging and distributors is correct. This question refers to the number of exhibitors rather than the number of visitors, so make sure that you are looking in the correct column. There are only two categories that add up to 13.

6 Answer **e** 100 is correct. This requires you to compare numbers (rather than percentages), i.e. 26% of 500 = 130, 16% of 190 = 30 then 130 − 30.

7 Answer **b** 45 is correct. Again, you are required to work out the numbers of staff in departments but this time, add them together.

8 Answer **c** Other is correct. This links percentages with fractions. One third is equivalent to 33.3% (100 ÷ 3) so the 34% shown in 'Other' is more than one third.

9 Answer **d** 370 is correct. Of the 500 permanent staff, 26% are employed in Production. As the question asks how many are not employed in Production, you must calculate the number in Production (26% of 500 = 130) and deduct this from the total number of permanent staff to get your answer.

10 Answer **c** 28 is correct. Work out the number of temporary staff in Customer Services (8) and in Sales and Marketing (20) and add together.

11 Answer **b** Production is correct. This is dealing only with percentages – no need to work out any figures. It is a direct comparison of the figures shown on the pie chart of permanent staff.

12 Answer **a** 100 is correct. One fifth is the equivalent of 20 per cent as shown on the chart, 500 ÷ 5 = 100.

13 Answer **c** 310 is correct. You do not need to use the charts for this – simply deduct the number of temporary staff from the number of permanent staff. These are shown as information extra to the charts, i.e. 500 − 190 = 310.

14 Answer **d** Personnel and Accounts is correct. Which departments add up to 6% in this chart? There are only two.

15 Answer **a** Personnel is correct. Note that this question asks for the smallest percentage – not necessarily the smallest number of staff. Where you are working with information from two, very similar charts, make sure you look at the correct chart as specified in the question.

16 Answer **d** 2005 is correct. Do not be waylaid by the irrelevant information supplied in the first sentence in this question. What you are required to do is contained just in the second sentence. 2005 is where the column representing monthly-paid staff is taller than the other column for the first time.

17 Answer **e** 140 is correct. Here you must add together the two columns taking care with the scale. For example, the reading midway between the two points for weekly-paid staff is 90.

18 Answer **a** 110 is correct. Deduct 30 (the figure for 2002) from 140 (2006).

19 Answer **d** 2005 is correct. Perhaps the easiest way to tackle this is to jot down the differences year by year – 40, 40, 30, 20, 40 – the only possible answer is then obvious.

20 Answer **d** 2005 is correct. As you can see, the weekly-paid staff membership increased from 2002 to 2004, decreased in 2005 and then stayed the same in 2006.

21 Answer **c** 2004 is correct. Reading the line that shows you details of Smith's Sales Company performance you will see that in 2002 they recorded a loss of £20,000 and in 2003 they were at breakeven (0). In 2004, however, they recorded their first positive profit (£14,000).

22 Answer **a** £30,000 is correct. With Jones' Jackets Ltd showing a profit of £25,000 in 2006, you should add

£5000 to this to arrive at the figure of 2006 profit plus 20%.

23 Answer **e** £3000 loss is correct. Here you must deal with negative figures. Jotting them down as you read them off the diagram might help, i.e. $-5, -6, +3, -1, +6 = -3$.

24 Answer **c** Peter's Parties is correct. Just look for the company whose line goes in a continually upwards direction.

25 Answer **a** Smith's Sales Company is correct. Here you should look for the line that goes upwards most steeply between one year and the next. Smith's Sales went from $-£20,000$ to 0 from 2002 to 2003.

TEST 7

ARITHMETIC

Questions 1 to 10 – Practice is the most effective way to improve your scores in this type of question. If you get any of these questions wrong, it might be useful to look back at the advice in the section of this chapter for Test 1 and then to attempt these questions again to see if your score has improved. If you still feel that you are not making progress, get help.

The answers in this type of question are usually quite straightforward – do not waste time looking for tricks or traps.

1 135

2 0

3 13

4 7

5 12

6 497

7 12

8 411

9 36

10 64

By this stage in your preparation, you may be finding the arithmetic sections relatively easy to do. However, they often get harder towards the end of the section so you will still need to work through them carefully. Do not forget, if you are finding yourself short of time – or you know that you usually work quite slowly – do the easiest ones first. This will give you confidence and also increase your chances of getting a better score.

11 Answer **b** 81 is correct. A simple addition.

12 Answer **c** 7 is correct. Knowing multiplication tables helps with this one.

13 Answer **e** 3.75 is correct. This is where the questions get a little more difficult – but do not panic, it is still straight-forward. Knowing that 0.5 $\times$ 0.5 (or $\frac{1}{2} \times \frac{1}{2}$) is 0.25 (or $\frac{1}{4}$) will help.

14 Answer **d** 75 is correct. This is a bit more involved but will still only test your ability to subtract. Work out the first half of the question $68 - 29 = 39$, then deduct that from the second part of the question $114 - 39 = 75$.

15 Answer **c** $\frac{2}{15}$ is correct. Fractions frighten many people but, with a basic understanding of fractions and a bit of practice, they can be quite simple. The key to this one is finding the common denominator. In this case it is 15 (3 $\times$ 5) and gives the calculation $\frac{5}{15} - \frac{3}{15}$ so the answer is $\frac{2}{15}$.

16 Answer **d** 12 is correct. Do not let the fact that this question is written differently put you off. All you have to do is divide 204 by 17 (remember that division is the opposite to multiplication) to get your answer. This is a typical example of the answer options being very similar. This precludes any estimation on your part – you just have to work it out.

17 Answer **e** 11 is correct. This is similar to the previous question. Just divide 132 by 12.

18 Answer **a** 28 is correct. This is a longer calculation but is very simple. Take the 13 from the sum of the numbers in the first part of the question.

19 Answer **e** 13 is correct. Again the answer from the first part must be used in the second part, i.e. $21 \div 3 = 7$, $91 \div 7 = 13$.

20 Answer **b** 14 is correct. Here, knowing the seven times table would be useful. If you can see at a glance that 3.5 is half of 7 and know that 7×7 is 49, then 2×7 will be your answer. Being able to use numbers quickly in this way is what questions like this are meant to test.

Questions 21 to 30 – With word problems of this type, practice will help you to focus on what the question requires. It does not matter if you are dealing with weights, measurements, amounts of money, time or any other quantity, you must always isolate the important bits of the question – perhaps by underlining them – and ignore the extra information you are given. Developing this ability to rapidly understand what is required will ensure that you get more questions of this type correct and also that you save time, giving you longer to spend on more difficult questions.

21 Answer **b** 36 kg is correct. Here you need to divide by 12 and multiply by 3. Alternatively you could divide by 4 to get the same answer. Just use whichever way you are most comfortable with.

22 Answer **d** £3 is correct. A simple division again, 81 ÷ 27 = 3.

23 Answer **d** £1536 is correct. 12 months at £128 per month is £1536.

24 Answer **e** 178 is correct. The calculation is £145 + £10 + £23 = £178.

25 Answer **a** £98,000 is correct. The large numbers may confuse you, causing you to make a mistake so ignore the three zeros while you get your answer quickly but do not forget to put them back.

26 Answer **c** 6'2" is correct. This is a straightforward addition so long as you do not forget that 12" = 1 foot!

27 Answer **e** $6\frac{1}{2}$ hours is correct. This is the perfect example of being given extra information that could confuse you.

Ignore the travelling time and the break and just concentrate on the actual hours worked.

28 Answer **b** 6 is correct. Just divide 15 by 2.5.

29 Answer **d** £4.25 is correct. Calculate how many 'blocks' of 3 minutes you would have to pay for, then multiply that by the rate per 3 minutes, i.e. $15 \div 3 = 5, 5 \times 0.85 = £4.25$.

30 Answer **d** £62,500 is correct. Subtract the deposit from the total price to get the outstanding balance.

The next ten questions ask you to estimate the answer. You need to choose the answer nearest to the correct one. You will need to work quickly and will obviously not be allowed to use a calculator. In estimating, you need to develop the skill of rounding up or down as appropriate to make your calculation easier and quicker. Your estimating skills can be greatly improved with practice so do plenty of sums involving mental arithmetic and practise estimating your shopping bill as you go around the supermarket, or play games involving scoring, such as darts or board games.

31 Answer **c** 19 is correct. By rounding up 0.8 to 1, you will quickly see that the correct answer must be about 24. However, do not leap in and choose 24 as your answer as you know that, having rounded up, the correct answer must be less than 24.

32 Answer **a** 120 is correct. 76% is so close to 75% – or $\frac{3}{4}$ – and 156 should be rounded up to 160. An estimation would therefore be $\frac{3}{4}$ of 160, i.e. 120.

33 Answer **e** 6 is correct. Here you just need to round up 29 to 30 then calculate one fifth of 30, i.e. 6.

34 Answer **b** 56 is correct. Do not let decimals worry you – they will round up or down in just the same way as whole numbers. So, 1.4 can be rounded up to 1.5 for the purposes of estimating the answer. $1\frac{1}{2}$ times 40 is 60 but you know that, having rounded up the 1.4, the answer must be less than 60.

35 Answer **a** 1900 is correct. A simple addition but do not forget that this exercise is to test your estimating skills – you may not find the exact answer in the choices given. Take care with choices **a** and **b** – they are close and fall either side of the correct answer if you were to calculate it exactly. The question you need to ask yourself, very quickly, is which of these two choices is the nearest. The 71 in the first number shows you that you should choose the higher figure.

36 Answer **c** −500 is correct. Here you are working with negative numbers but this should not make any difference to your ability to estimate. Roughly work out the correct answer then see which of the choices given is nearest.

37 Answer **d** 4700 is correct. As you know, 50% is equivalent to $\frac{1}{2}$ so divide by 2 to get an answer, but for speed do not be tempted to work it out exactly – remember to estimate!

38 Answer **b** £76 is correct. To estimate the answer to this question, you would add together the pounds figures only. However, when the answer choices are quite close together, as in this question, you need to take extra care to estimate accurately.

39 Answer **d** 1080 is correct. 89% is obviously very nearly 90% so simply deduct 10%, i.e. $1200 - 120 = 1080$.

40 Answer **a** £3.75 is correct. Unless you are unusual and can work out $\frac{3}{16}$ in your head, you will need to see that $\frac{3}{16}$ is midway between $\frac{1}{4}(\frac{4}{16})$ and $\frac{1}{8}(\frac{2}{16})$ of £20, i.e. midway between £5 and £2.50.

TEST 8

PERCENTAGES, FRACTIONS AND SEQUENCES

1 Answer **e** 25 is correct. The calculation is $32 \div 8 = 4$, i.e. $\frac{1}{4}$, and a quarter is equivalent to 25%.

2 Answer **b** $\frac{1}{4}$ is correct, i.e. $\frac{1}{2} \div 2 = \frac{1}{4}$.

3 Answer **c** 0.01 is correct. Finding 10% is the same as finding one tenth or dividing by 10 so move the decimal point one place to the left to get your answer.

4 Answer **d** $\frac{7}{8}$ is correct. The common denominator here is 8 so express all the fractions in eighths, i.e. $\frac{2}{8} + \frac{4}{8} + \frac{1}{8} = \frac{7}{8}$.

5 Answer **c** 20 is correct. Tackle this question in two parts, i.e. 50% of $400 = 200$, then 10% of $200 = 20$.

6 Answer **a** 4050 is correct. Your calculations should be $10125 \div 5 = 2025$ $(\frac{1}{5})$ then $2025 \times 2 = 4050$ $(\frac{2}{5})$.

7 Answer **b** £92 is correct. To work out 40% you should divide by 10 then multiply by 4.

8 Answer **e** £115.50 is correct. If 10% of 110 is 11, then 5% is £5.50 then do not forget to add the £110 to get your answer.

9 Answer **b** 18 is correct. Knowing multiplication tables helps with this one. $(81 \div 9) \times 2 = 18$.

10 Answer **c** $1\frac{2}{3}$ is correct. As with most fraction questions, you need to find the common denominator. Here it is 9 so $\frac{3}{9} + \frac{2}{9} = \frac{5}{9}$, then $\times 3 = \frac{15}{9}$. Reduce this down to correctly state the fraction as $1\frac{2}{3}$.

11 The answer is 63. To get 50% you must divide by 2.

12 The answer is 600. You are being asked to find the rejected amount so 20% of 3000 = $3000 \div 5 = 600$.

13 The answer is 41. To find a third you must divide 123 by 3.

14 The answer is 9 minutes. 10 minutes less 10% = 9.

15 The answer is 4%. You are being asked to express 2 as a percentage of 50, i.e. $\frac{2}{50} = \frac{4}{100} = 4\%$.

16 The answer is £90. The quickest way to answer this is 2 printers at £50 each = £100, less 10% = £90.

17 The answer is £112. Understanding the relation that percentages have to fractions makes this question easier. If you know that $12\frac{1}{2}\%$ is the same as one eighth, then work out $\frac{1}{8}$ of £128 = £16. £128 less the reduction of £16 = £112.

18 The answer is 311. To work out 25% (the proportion of staff who are men) you should divide the total staff number by 4.

19 The answer is £48,000. The calculation here is 120,000 ÷ 5 × 2 = 48,000.

20 The answer is $\frac{1}{3}$. 24 ÷ 8 = 3, i.e. one third.

21 Answer **b** 4 is correct. Each number is doubled.

22 Answer **b** 11 is correct. Deduct 2 each time.

23 Answer **c** $\frac{5}{15}$ is correct. This is simpler than it looks. The numerator (the number at the top of the fraction) has been increased by one each time and the denominator (the number at the bottom) has been increased by 3.

24 Answer **c** 6 is correct. Here, 1.5 is added each time.

25 Answer **a** 9 is correct. When you have worked out the difference between each pair of numbers, you should see that the pattern here is add 1, then add 2, add 1, add 2.

26 Answer **d** 17 is correct. The pattern here is subtracting a number decreasing by one each time, and when reaching zero starting to add one, i.e. − 3, − 2, − 1, − 0 + 1.

27 Answer **d** 28 is correct. The amount added between each pair of numbers increases by 2 each time, i.e. + 6, + 8, + 10, + 12.

28 Answer **a** 22 is correct. This one has a more unusual pattern. Between the first two numbers 2 is added, then that number is doubled, then 2 is added, then the number is doubled again.

29 Answer **c** 13 is correct. Here is another unusual pattern. Each time the previous two numbers add up to the third one so 2 + 3 = 5, 5 + 3 = 8 and so on.

30 Answer **a** −1 is correct. If you have not been able to 'see' this pattern, try writing down the numbers shown in the question and answers in the sequence in which you would normally see them, i.e. −1, 0, 1, 2, 3, 4, 5, then follow how the question sequence moves around the normal sequence. It moves from 2 to 3 then back to 1, up to 4 then down to 0, up to 5 − it is moving further out from the starting point by 1 each time, backwards and forwards − the next number if we carried on this sequence would be 6, then 2 and so on.

31 Answer **c** 6 is correct. This is an easy one to start this section − all the numbers are odd with the exception of 6 which should, of course, be 5 to make the correct sequence.

32 Answer **d** 104 is correct. The number to be added to the preceding digit increases by one each time.

33 Answer **d** 4535 is correct. Do not let the larger numbers deter you. If necessary you can ignore the first two digits of each number, as they remain the same throughout the sequence. Concentrate on the last two digits and you will see that the numbers decrease by 11, then 12, then 13 and so on.

34 Answer **e** +2 is correct. Despite the presence of negative numbers this is straightforward. It is the most familiar sequence − counting − but it starts from −4. The last figure should therefore be +1.

35 Answer **b** 36 is correct. By the time you get to the fifth figure in this sequence you should be able to see that the pattern is ÷ 2 then × 4, ÷ 2, × 4, ÷ 2 and the correct figure would be 32.

36 Answer **a** 620 is correct. Each number is multiplied by a figure that increases by one each time, i.e. $\times$ 2, $\times$ 3, $\times$ 4 etc.

37 Answer **b** 2 is correct. The sequence is $+$ 5, $\times$ 2, $+$ 5, $\times$ 2 and so on, making the correct number to start the sequence 1.

38 Answer **c** 4 is correct. This is a common type of sequence – the number to be added increases by one each time.

39 Answer **d** 41 is correct. The sequence is followed by adding 4 each time but the last figure is wrong because 6 has been added.

40 Answer **c** 8 is correct. The sequence here is $-$ 3, $-$ 2, $-$ 3, $-$ 2, $-$ 3 but, in the middle of the sequence, 2 is subtracted rather than 3.

TEST 9

INFORMATION FROM CHARTS AND TABLES

Questions testing your ability to obtain information from tables of figures are often quite easy. You must read the question carefully so that you can home in on the relevant information – the correct column and so on.

1 Answer **b** 1152 is correct. This is a straightforward addition of the appropriate column.

2 Answer **e** 6 hours is correct. Here you must find the total number of complaints and then multiply by the length of the call, i.e. 30 $\times$ 12 = 360 minutes = 6 hours.

3 Answer **e** 16 is correct. Ignore Susan's total in the complaint calls column and add up the remaining people's calls in that column.

4 Answer **b** 155 is correct. Take Jo's total calls from Mark's, i.e. $322 - 167 = 155$.

5 Answer **e** Tony is correct. Look in the product enquiries column for the highest figure.

6 Answer **d** £7,200 is correct. The total amount spent on promotional activities was £80,000 and stationery represented 9% of this. You are therefore being asked to calculate 9% of £80,000.

7 Answer **c** 53p is correct. Firstly calculate 33% of £80,000 then divide by 50,000 to get the cost per brochure. Note that the question asks for the approximate cost – the precise answer would be slightly under 53p.

8 Answer **b** 300,000 is correct. This is a similar question to the previous one but asked the opposite way. The calculation is 15% of £80,000 divided by 4p but there is a common pitfall here. You must remember to take care to divide by £0.04 and not just by 4.

9 Answer **d** Leaflets is correct. As $\frac{1}{4}$ is the same as 25%, you simply have to look for the category in the pie chart shown as 25%.

10 Answer **a** £88,000 is correct. The information for this answer is shown outside the pie chart. You are told that the cost over the year is £80,000 and 10% added to this will give you the new budget figure.

The next five questions are based on information contained in a column chart. A stacked column chart can be, as in this case, a version of the more usual column chart that you have seen in previous sections or it could also be used to show the figures as percentages of the total figure represented by the column – similar to the way pie charts do. The information given in the key and titles will give you the details you need to understand which approach is being taken.

11 Answer **b** £20,000 is correct. The only information you need to note from the first sentence in this question is the year. The calculation is $(145 - 65) - (115 - 55) = 80 - 60 = 20$.

12 Answer **d** £140,000 is correct. Read off the value at the top of the stacked column for 2004.

13 Answer **c** £40,000 is correct. The figures to be used in this question go from 95 to 135. Therefore this represents a profit for this department of £40,000.

14 Answer **d** 2006 is correct. A quick visual check should show you the answer here but a more detailed look at the actual profit figures shown on the chart will confirm your answer if you are in any doubt.

15 Answer **a** £90,000 is correct. Here you are being asked to add together the figures relating to ornamental china together – take note that there are only 3 years that are relevant to this question.

16 Answer **b** $700 million is correct. There is no trick here – it is simply a test of your ability to work accurately with figures in a line diagram so take care to select the correct year and so on. Read off the two values for the appropriate year and subtract one from the other to get the correct answer.

17 Answer **b** $1120 million is correct. This is a straight-forward percentage calculation using figures from the diagram. If you are not allowed to use a calculator for this type of problem, remember that 20% is another way of expressing one fifth. Simply find the right figure on the diagram and subtract one fifth to represent the 20% fall in imports.

18 Answer **a** France and Italy is correct. You should quickly be able to spot that only two lines go down rather than up or across – these are the lines for the two countries you are looking for.

19 Answer **c** $500 million is correct. In 2006 the UK spent $1400, while France spent $900 million.

20 Answer **e** $100 million is correct. Locate the correct line for Italy and the relevant years. The amount spent went from $800 million to half way between 800 and 600, i.e. 700.

TEST 10

MIXED TEST

1 404

2 4416

3 5885

4 66

5 b 3545

6 e £2.45

7 c 12p

8 a £495

9 e 1250

10 d 3300

The first ten questions in this mixed test are quite straightforward – they are just testing your ability to use the four mathematical operations – addition, subtraction, multiplication and division. There are no tricks, although in the multiple-choice questions – for example question 5 – many of the answers will be similar, so you will have to be careful when making your selection. Guessing will not help in this case. If you are still having problems in this area, get hold of a good basic arithmetic book and practise, practise, practise.

Questions 11 to 20 involve fractions, percentages, decimals and number sequences. Let's look at some specific explanations:

11 Answer **c** 90 is correct. Simply divide 405 by 9 then multiply by 2.

12 Answer **e** $\frac{3}{4}$ is correct. This question checks your understanding of the relation between fractions and decimals and should pose you no problems. If you have difficulty, try making yourself a list of fractions – $\frac{1}{6}$, $\frac{1}{5}$, $\frac{1}{4}$, $\frac{1}{3}$, $\frac{1}{2}$, $\frac{2}{3}$ and so on. Note the decimal equivalent by the side then study this before any test.

13 Answer **a** 210 is correct. Here you could divide by 100 and multiply by 35 to get your answer.

14 Answer **d** 165 is correct. Here you must read the question carefully. It asks how many of the employees are men. You are told that 25% are women so don't be tempted to work out 25% – answer **a** would be correct if that were the question. You must calculate 75%.

15 Answer **b** 0.03 is correct. For this question you need to understand that the first digit after the decimal point represents tenths and the second digit is hundredths, so three hundredths is expressed as 0.03. Take care with this as many of the answers are similar.

The next five questions involve number sequences where you must spot a pattern in the progression of the list of numbers. For this type of question it is usually a good idea to jot down the difference between each pair of numbers in the sequence.

16 Answer **e** 40 is correct. The difference between each pair of numbers increases by 3 each time i.e. -3, -6, -9 and so on.

17 Answer **b** 29 is correct. In this sequence, 5 is added to the preceding number each time.

18 Answer **a** 184 is correct. The number is doubling each time.

19 Answer **e** 124 is correct. This is a perfect example of where jotting down the difference between each pair of numbers in a sequence will help you. The differences are +3, +5, +7, +9, +11 so you can see that you should add 13 to get your answer.

20 Answer **c** 87 is correct. Here the numbers are decreasing by 6 each time.

21 Answer **c** 165 is correct. Here you should multiply the average number of employees in catering businesses by the number of catering businesses i.e. 15 × 11.

22 Answer **d** 69 is correct. This is simply a matter of adding up the figures in the column headed 'No. of businesses in category'.

23 Answer **e** 383 is correct. For this you need to work out the number of people working in call centres, i.e. 130, and add this to the number working for the local authority.

24 Answer **a** Manufacturing is correct. Obviously, the local authority is the single largest employer – but that is not the question. You must multiply the average number of employees in each type of business by the number of that type of businesses that took part in the survey.

25 Answer **b** 1933 is correct. Here you are being asked for the total number of people employed by all the businesses. Don't fall into the trap of simply adding up the figures in the column showing the average number of employees per business (answer **d** is there for those who make that mistake). You must calculate the number of employees in each type of business then add your five totals together to get the correct answer.

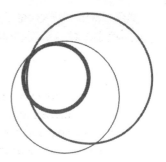

CHAPTER FOUR
DIAGNOSIS AND
FURTHER READING

Now that you have done the tests, how can you work out your score and evaluate your performance? Hopefully you will have found that the extensive practice has helped and that you have improved as you have gone through the timed tests. So let us look at what happens next.

Finding out your actual score is interesting but it is not the most important aspect. It is more meaningful to find out whether your score is above or below average. This is what a prospective employer will do. They will compare your score with the scores obtained by people similar to you. According to the test criteria, these people – your peer group – may be similar in age, educational level, job status and so on. Obviously, you cannot do this to any great extent if there is just you involved in the testing process, but an elementary marking scheme and evaluation grid is shown here so that you can get an idea of your basic aptitude for numerical reasoning.

Before you go ahead with evaluating your score, it is important to understand that each psychometric test has its own scoring system and there is really no way for you to know exactly how the test is scored before you start. Some tests will award extra points for attempting all the questions. Others will deduct points for incorrect answers. However, a common feature of all tests is the standardisation of your score relative to other candidates in your peer group. You cannot judge your aptitude simply by knowing your own raw score. This is because scores must be compared with those of other candidates and also because not all scores are used by employers in the same way. An employer may use the tests to choose the best from a group of candidates, while another may have a target score in mind and may accept for interview all candidates who reach that score.

If you have taken a comprehensive set of tests to assess your abilities in a number of areas, it may be that a profile chart will be put together by the people administering the tests. This will plot your relative high and low scores across different areas and may be used to judge to which type of job you are best suited. In any event, it may be worth requesting feedback if you have taken part in this type of assessment.

DIAGNOSIS

This basic marking scheme is an example of how a raw score may be used to evaluate a candidate's relative aptitude and the element of comparison is an important point to understand. If members of your peer group get, on average, a score of 80 or more in a test, then your score of 75 will be a poor one whereas if your peer group gains average scores of 70 or less, then your score of 75 would be above average.

So, go through each test that you have completed. Mark each answer as correct or incorrect and note any to which you were unable to give an answer. Each question correctly answered scores 5 marks as follows.

Correct answers	1	2	3	4	5	6	7	8	9	10
Score	5	10	15	20	25	30	35	40	45	50

Incorrect answers score zero points.

Now, for each question that you did not attempt, deduct two marks from your final 'correct marks' score as follows:

Questions not attempted	1	2	3	4	5	6	7	8	9	10
Deducted marks	2	4	6	8	10	12	14	16	18	20

For example, 36 questions correct, 2 incorrect, 2 not attempted, would score as follows:

36 correct $\times$ 5 marks = 180
2 incorrect $\times$ 0 marks = 0
2 incomplete $\times$ -2 = -4
'Raw' test score = 180 $-$ 4 = 176

(NB Each test will have a potential score according to the number of questions in that particular test, of course.)

You will have a separate score for each of the tests – do not add these together but use them to chart your progress as you have gone through the book.

Now use the following table according to the number of questions in the tests to interpret your final score for each test:

Number of questions in test	Well below average	Below average	Average	Above average	Well above average
20	0 to 30	31 to 49	50 to 60	61 to 84	85 or over
25	0 to 35	36 to 59	60 to 75	76 to 104	105 or over
35	0 to 45	46 to 84	85 to 105	106 to 144	145 or over
40	0 to 50	51 to 99	100 to 125	126 to 164	165 or over

If your score is 'Above average' or 'Well above average', you may decide that you would like to spend more of your preparation time on other sections of the tests you may sit – maybe the Verbal Reasoning, or Diagrammatic Reasoning. If the results indicate that your score is average or below, get some help with the basics of numeracy before your test.

Whatever your score, do not allow yourself to be discouraged – tests are only part of the interview process and it is possible to improve with practice.

SUGGESTIONS FOR FURTHER IMPROVEMENT

Remember that your own reactions to your performance in the tests are subjective. You are quite often not the best judge of your own performance. It might help you if you can get some feedback about your results from the test administrators. However, this is sometimes difficult to obtain as it is a time-consuming task for employers to undertake.

Above all, keep an open mind. You can improve and your dislike of Maths at school does not have to last for the rest of your life. The obvious incentive for you to undertake all this extra effort is the job you really want and the salary you deserve.

ON THE DAY

You must plan to arrive at the test centre in a state that is conducive to achieving your best possible score. This means being calm and focused. It is possible that you may feel nervous before the test, but you can help yourself by preparing in advance the practical details that will enable you to do well. Remember, it is unlikely that you are the only person who is feeling nervous; what is important is how you deal with your nerves! The following suggestions may help you to overcome unnecessary test-related anxiety.

1 Know where the test centre is located, and estimate how long it will take you to get there – plan your 'setting off time'. Now plan to leave 45 minutes before your setting off time to allow for travel delays. This way, you can be more or less certain that you will arrive at the test centre in good time. If, for any reason, you think you will miss the start of the session, call the administrator to ask for instructions.

2 Try to get a good night's sleep before the test. This is obvious advice and, realistically, it is not always possible, particularly if you are prone to nerves the night before a test. However, you can take some positive steps to help. Consider taking a hot bath before you go to bed, drinking herbal rather than caffeinated tea, and doing some exercise. Think back to what worked last time you took an exam and try to replicate the scenario.

3 The night before the test, organise everything that you need to take with you. This includes test instructions, directions, your identification, pens, erasers, possibly your

calculator (with new batteries in it), reading glasses, and contact lenses.

4 Decide what you are going to wear and have your clothes ready the night before. Be prepared for the test centre to be unusually hot or cold, and dress in layers so that you can regulate the climate yourself. If your test will be preceded or followed by an interview, make sure you dress accordingly for the interview which is likely to be a more formal event than the test itself.

5 Eat breakfast! Even if you usually skip breakfast, you should consider that insufficient sugar levels affect your concentration and that a healthy breakfast might help you to concentrate, especially towards the end of the test when you are likely to be tired.

6 If you know that you have specific or exceptional requirements which will require preparation on the day, be sure to inform the test administrators in advance so that they can assist you as necessary. This may include wheelchair access, the availability of the test in Braille, or a facility for those with hearing difficulties. Similarly, if you are feeling unusually unwell on the day of the test, make sure that the test administrator is aware of it.

7 If, when you read the test instructions, there is something you don't understand, ask for clarification from the administrator. The time given to you to read the instructions may or may not be limited but, within the allowed time, you can usually ask questions. Don't assume that you have understood the instructions if, at first glance, they appear to be similar to the instructions for the practice tests.

8 Don't read through all the questions before you start. This simply wastes time. Start with Question 1 and work swiftly and methodically through each question in order. Unless you are taking a computerised test where the level of difficulty of the next question depends on you correctly answering the previous question (such as the GMAT or GRE), don't waste time on questions that you know require a lot of time. You can return to these questions at the end if you have time left over.

9 After you have taken the test, find out the mechanism for feedback, and approximately the number of days you will have to wait to find out your results. Ask whether there is scope for objective feedback on your performance for your future reference.

10 Celebrate that you have finished.

FURTHER SOURCES OF PRACTICE

In this final section, you will find a list of useful sources for all types of psychometric tests.

BOOKS

Bolles, Richard N., *What Color Is Your Parachute?* Berkeley, CA: Ten Speed Press, 2007.

Carter, P. and K. Russell, *Psychometric Testing: 1000 Ways to Assess Your Personality, Creativity, Intelligence and Lateral Thinking*. Chichester: John Wiley, 2001.

Jackson, Tom, *The Perfect Résumé*. New York: Broadway Books, 2004.

Kourdi, Jeremy, *Succeed at Psychometric Testing: Practice Tests for Verbal Reasoning Advanced*. London: Hodder Education, 2008.

Krannich, Ronald L. and Caryl Rae Krannich, *Network Your Way to Job and Career Success*. Manassa, VA: Impact Publications, 1989.

Nuga, Simbo, *Succeed at Psychometric Testing: Practice Tests for Verbal Reasoning Intermediate*. London: Hodder Education, 2008.

Rhodes, Peter, *Succeed at Psychometric Testing: Practice Tests for Critical Verbal Reasoning*. London: Hodder Education, 2008.

Rhodes, Peter, *Succeed at Psychometric Testing: Practice Tests for Diagrammatic and Abstract Reasoning*. London: Hodder Education, 2008.

Vanson, Sally, *Succeed at Psychometric Testing: Practice Tests for Data Interpretation*. London: Hodder Education, 2008.

Walmsley, Bernice, *Succeed at Psychometric Testing: Practice Tests for Numerical Reasoning Advanced*. London: Hodder Education, 2008.

Walmsley, Bernice, *Succeed at Psychometric Testing: Practice Tests for the National Police Selection Process*. London: Hodder Education, 2008.

TEST PUBLISHERS AND SUPPLIERS

ASE
Chiswick Centre
414 Chiswick High Road
London W4 5TF
telephone: 0208 996 3337
www.ase-solutions.co.uk

Hogrefe Ltd
Burgner House
4630 Kingsgate
Oxford Business Park South
Oxford OX4 2SU
telephone: 01865 402900
www.hogrefe.co.uk

Oxford Psychologists Press
Elsfield Hall
15–17 Elsfield Way
Oxford OX2 8EP
telephone: 01865 404500
www.opp.co.uk

Pearson
Assessment
Halley Court
Jordan Hill
Oxford OX2 8EJ
telephone: 01865 888188
www.pearson-uk.com

SHL
The Pavilion
1 Atwell Place
Thames Ditton
Surrey KT7 0SR
telephone: 0208 398 4170
www.shl.com

OTHER USEFUL WEBSITES

Websites are prone to change, but the following are correct at the time of going to press.

www.careerpsychologycentre.com

www.cipd.org.uk

www.deloitte.co.uk/index.asp

www.ets.org

www.freesat1prep.com

www.mensa.org.uk

www.morrisby.co.uk

www.newmonday.co.uk

www.oneclickhr.com

www.pgcareers.com/apply/how/recruitment.asp

www.psychtesting.org.uk

www.psychtests.com

www.publicjobs.gov.ie

www.puzz.com

www.testagency.co.uk

www.tests-direct.com

OTHER USEFUL ORGANISATIONS

American Psychological Association Testing and Assessment – www.apa.org/science/testing

Association of Recognised English Language Schools (ARELS) – www.englishuk.com

Australian Psychological Society – www.psychology.org.au

The Best Practice Club – www.bpclub.com

The British Psychological Society – www.bps.org.uk

Canadian Psychological Association – www.cpa.ca

The Chartered Institute of Marketing – www.cim.co.uk

The Chartered Institute of Personnel and Development – www.cipd.co.uk

The Chartered Management Institute – www.managers.org.uk

Psyconsult – www.psyconsult.co.uk

Singapore Psychological Society – www.singaporepsychologicalsociety.co.uk

Society for Industrial and Organisational Assessment (South Africa) (SIOPSA) – www.siposa.org.za